Folio

778.9
Mel

Meltzer, Milton
The eye of conscience

THE EYE OF CONSCIENCE

THE EYE OF CONSCIENCE

Photographers and Social Change

with 100 photographs by noted photographers, past and present

by MILTON MELTZER and BERNARD COLE

FOLLETT PUBLISHING COMPANY   Chicago

Jacket photo by Lewis W. Hine
Workers in a Pennsylvania coal mine, 1911.

Appreciation is expressed to the following persons and organizations
for permission to reproduce photographs:
Michael Abramson, pages 141-50.
Morrie Camhi, pages 172-81.
The Jacob A. Riis Collection, Museum of the City of New York, pages 39-48.
Fung Lam, pages 128-37.
Library of Congress, (Lewis W. Hine) cover and pages 58-67;
    (Dorothea Lange) pages 82-91;
    (Timothy O'Sullivan) pages 21-30.
William (Bill) Mackey, Jr., pages 96-105.
Ira Nowinski, pages 156-65.
Martin Schneider, *Life,* pages 113-22.

To Gwen and Rebecca

CONTENTS

ACKNOWLEDGMENTS

Our thanks first of all to the six contemporary photographers who permitted us to publish their photographs and who submitted patiently to nagging questions about their life and work. For access to the photographic files of the work of O'Sullivan, Hine, and Lange and for help in obtaining prints, we are grateful to Jerry Kearns, head of the reference service of the Library of Congress, and to the staff of that department. For the Riis photographs, our thanks go to Charlotte LaRue of the Museum of the City of New York.

For permission to use material from interviews with Dorothea Lange conducted by Suzanne Riess of the Regional Oral History Office, the Bancroft Library, University of California, Berkeley, we extend our appreciation to Willa Baum, Department Head, to Dr. Paul Taylor, who checked our manuscript, and to the Photo Library of the Museum of Modern Art, New York City, for letting us use its copy of the transcribed interviews. Other sources of information about all of the photographers represented in this book may be found in the reading list at the back.

We also give thanks to John Wiley and Sons for permission to use copyrighted material from *Springboards* about Lewis Hine and Jacob Riis, written by Milton Meltzer, and we gratefully acknowledge the permission of the *New Yorker* and the artist to reprint the Alan Dunn cartoon that opens the last chapter. Finally, our warmest thanks to Sandra Greifenstein, whose editorial intelligence and concern saw this book through from conception to birth.

MILTON MELTZER
BERNARD COLE

INTRODUCTION

How easy it was to stand by and say nothing while one hundred and ten thousand Japanese-Americans were illegally stripped of their rights and penned up in prison camps for the duration of World War II.

In the strange, almost paranoid way we sometimes behave, the same government agency charged with executing this unconstitutional policy hired Dorothea Lange to photograph the travesty of justice. Her pictures today, more than thirty years after the event, document the facts of the crime and let us share the feelings of the victims.

Perhaps no other photographer could have been better for this work. "She functioned," wrote the *New York Times,* "in effect as our national eye of conscience in the internment camps. Her constant concerns—the survival of human dignity under impossible conditions, the confrontation of the system by the individual, and the helpless innocence of children—were perfectly suited to the subject . . ."

It is that kind of photography which this book is about. From the beginning of the art—and it is a young one—some photographers have confronted the life around them and shared the truths they saw. Although they were often concerned to document a single event or condition of existence, their photographs remind us of our common humanity. Behind the lens was a personal vision of what life is and what it could be. They hoped to make it better, to change the world by their exposure of the truth.

The work of ten such photographers is represented here. The first four—O'Sullivan, Riis, Hine, and Lange—are among the great pioneers. The other six—Mackey, Schneider, Lam, Abramson, Nowinski, and Camhi—are chosen from among the many at work today. They can all be called documentary photographers, but because they are artists too, the images they make are of permanent interest. As art, they exist for their own sake.

From the hundreds and sometimes thousands of pictures made in the course of probing a single issue or theme, we have selected ten to represent each photographer's work. It is an unfairly small fraction. But the object was to show a variety of ways to work, and to indicate, through the biographical sketches, the many paths by which these men and women came to find their greatest challenge.

This book, then, has another purpose—to help you express what you feel and think through the camera. It is not a technical manual, although a great deal about what it takes to make superb photographs can be found in these pages. No, it has more to do with exploring yourself and the world around you. It is about awareness and growth. It is about finding your own way to see, and expanding your insight into human existence.

TIMOTHY O'SULLIVAN

In the long blue columns making a forced march north along
the Pennsylvania roads to catch up with Lee's marauders,
there was a small wagon with canvas sides. It was both home
and darkroom for Timothy O'Sullivan. Inside, the twenty-two-
year-old photographer stored his plates, chemicals, and the
few personal belongings a man could cling to at the front.
In good weather it was better to sleep under the wagon. When
it rained or snowed and he could find no room in tent or shed,
he was forced to sleep inside the smelly darkroom.

Now, in the early summer of 1863, the Army of the Potomac
was trying to halt the Confederate invasion of Pennsylvania.
So fast had General Robert E. Lee's men swept north that
clerks in Washington, D. C., were preparing to burn official
records for fear the gray tide would soon flood into the capital.
On the morning of July 1, as Confederate skirmishers crossed
a pike a few miles from a town called Gettysburg, they ran
into Union cavalrymen and a few shots were exchanged. The
battle of Gettysburg was begun.

For three bloody days the fighting went on. At the end Lee
escaped into Virginia, but left about four thousand of his men
dead on the battlefield and about twenty-four thousand
wounded or missing. Hundreds of writers have had their say
about Gettysburg, from Lincoln's memorable few words to

Catton's vivid volumes, but nothing makes that battlefield as real as Timothy O'Sullivan's photographs. With his camera he moved wherever the action was—the wheat field, Little Round Top, Devil's Den, Torstle's barn, General Meade's headquarters.

It was O'Sullivan's "most reliable" war pictures that *Harper's* rushed to the nation together with the report of the battle. Farmers in their barns, mechanics at their workbenches, mothers in their kitchens, knew now what war meant for their sons. Here, in one photograph, the young men lazing about the campfire, smiling into the camera; and here, a day later, the corpses stiffly silent. Mistakenly, however, credit for the pictures was given to the nation's best-known photographer, Mathew W. Brady. And it is Brady's name that has been identified in the public mind with Civil War photography. Not until recent years, chiefly as a result of James Horan's research for his books on Brady, has the significance of the "T. O'Sullivan" credit line been recognized.

O'Sullivan was born in Ireland, probably in 1839. That was the year the Frenchman Louis Daguerre invented the process by which pictures could be produced on the face of a copper plate. Daguerre's technique for making pictures was not complicated. He coated one side of a clean, polished sheet of copper with silver. Then he exposed this surface to iodine vapors in a small box at ordinary temperatures. In from five to thirty seconds the silvered side turned a golden yellow. He then placed the sensitized plate in the camera for a period of five to ten minutes in summer, or five to twelve minutes in winter. He developed the negative by exposing it in a closed box to mercury vapors heated to 167 degrees Fahrenheit. Finally the plate was washed with hyposulphite of soda.

The result astonished and delighted the world. Samuel F. B. Morse, inventor of the telegraph, saw the new "daguerreotypes" in Paris and wrote home that the "exquisite minuteness of the delineation cannot be conceived." The 5x7-inch fixed images that came from the daguerreotype camera "are Rembrandt perfected," he said. That fall Morse returned to New York with a daguerreotype camera made to his order, and when he exhibited the views it took, American photography was launched. Within the year photographers were opening studios in New York and other cities.

It was then that two-year-old Timothy O'Sullivan was brought by his mother and father to New York. With thousands of others they were fleeing the famine that the potato blight had inflicted upon Ireland. The O'Sullivan family settled on Staten Island.

While still a boy, Timothy found a job in Manhattan running errands for Mathew Brady. Brady, an upstate New Yorker, had opened a photography gallery on Fulton Street and Broadway in 1844, probably after learning the daguerreotype technique from attending Morse's public lectures. The energetic Brady, only twenty-one when he entered photography, won prizes early for his skill and quickly established a flourishing studio. Soon his prestige brought to his door celebrated Americans who were curious to have their portraits made by the new photographic process. By the end of the decade he was taking the pictures of almost every notable contemporary figure— presidents, generals, diplomats, artists, writers, statesmen, and business leaders.

By 1850, suffering from steadily deteriorating vision, Brady was obliged to rely on the operators he hired and trained. His profitable studio gave him the funds to experiment with new equipment while maintaining the high quality of his art. Now it was no longer possible to tell who deserved the credit for the work that carried the Brady credit line. His name only was stamped on every daguerreotype or paper print, a custom followed almost universally by the rivals who succeeded in building up large studios.

In the 1850s a way was found to make woodcut illustrations from daguerreotypes. The result was exciting and brought the new art before the large audiences who read the national weeklies such as *Harper's* and *Leslie's.* More important, however, was the invention of the wet plate in 1851 by the English sculptor Frederick Scott Archer. It revolutionized photography. Archer used collodion to keep the image on the glass plate. The sticky mixture of ether and alcohol evaporated quickly, leaving a smooth transparent film, sensitized by a bath in a solution of silver nitrate. The plate had to be used wet, while the sensitivity lasted. A method was soon developed to give the prints a glossy look by dipping the paper into a salt solution to which albumen was added. By 1853 paper photography was replacing the daguerreotype at Brady's and all other studios.

That same year the O'Sullivans bought a house at Castleton Corners, on Staten Island, near Brady's home. There were other pioneer photographers living on the rural island then, and it is possible that young O'Sullivan heard the new art discussed by them or even learned the technique from one of them. At any rate, a niece of Brady's said it was her uncle who taught the boy how to be a photographer.

In 1851 Brady appointed Alexander Gardner, an accomplished photographer from Scotland, to manage the Brady gallery in Washington, D. C. O'Sullivan, then one of Brady's apprentices, was asked to go along. From Gardner, O'Sullivan learned to be highly proficient in every phase of development that photography was rapidly going through. He handled the different cameras and made not only daguerreotypes and paper photographs but also the new ambrotypes, tintypes, and cartes de visite. When a stereo camera made it possible to produce four or more negatives on one glass plate, hundreds of thousands of prints began to pour out of the studios. Ordinary people could build their own portrait collections by buying prints of the famous from such studios as Brady's.

To Brady goes the credit for determining to photograph the American Civil War. He was not the first to carry a camera to the battlefield, however. A daguerreotypist, whose name is lost, took photos of troops in the Mexican War of the 1840s, but not when they were in combat. And the Englishman Roger Fenton went to the Crimean War in 1855 to photograph soldiers and battlefield landscapes. In contrast to the romantic battle scenes made by painters, these pictures were authentic witness to the reality seen by the soldiers, however limited by the camera's inability to catch armies in action.

Brady's goal was more ambitious. He had tried for years to record current history with his camera. Because of the technical limitations of photography, he was confined to portraits of illustrious Americans. History in motion, the upheavals of society, could not be captured by the lens because of the long exposure required. Still, if Brady could get in the thick of the fighting, he could document the effects of war in all its violence and savagery. It meant risking his life; it meant sacrificing a commercial success for an experiment in pictorial war reporting. All Lincoln would give him was his signature to a scrap of paper that read "Pass Brady." And not a penny to go with it. If he would photograph the war, it had to be at his own expense.

When the first blood was drawn, at Bull Run, there was Brady, dapper in his broadcloth suit, linen duster, and wide-brimmed hat, photographing the retreating Union troops and the terrified citizens scrambling away from a battle they had come out from Washington to see as though it were a charming new spectator sport. "His groupings of entire regiments and divisions, within a space of a couple of feet square," said *Humphrey's Journal,* "present some of the most curious effects as yet produced in photography. Considering the circumstances under which they were taken, amidst the excitement, the rapid movements, and the smoke of the battlefield, there is nothing to compare with them in their powerful contrasts of light and shade."

Before the year was out Brady had recruited photography

teams for most of the theaters of war. Little is known of many of his cameramen—only their names. Gardner was one who worked with a Brady darkroom wagon in the early stages of the war. It is hard to trace O'Sullivan's movements for the same period. After the war he referred to the First Battle of Bull Run in a way that makes it seem likely he had been with Brady and possibly had taken some of the photos credited to his employer.

By November, 1861, O'Sullivan was with the Union forces who occupied Port Royal and the Sea Islands of South Carolina. He was now working for Gardner, who was attached to General George B. McClellan's Army of the Potomac. Gardner had left Brady and set up his own shop. Some three hundred photographers, the record shows, received passes to shoot the war. Some made money out of it, selling their negatives to E. and H. T. Anthony, New York publishers who printed the pictures as cartes de visite and sold them by the thousands.

O'Sullivan, like all the others, had to overcome great difficulties to get his war pictures. He needed to win the cooperation of commanding officers wherever he went. Then he had to make his own way to the scene of battle. And always he had to cope with the problems of maintaining adequate and fresh supplies, and of transporting the heavy but fragile glass plates (mostly 8x10 inches) and the bulky equipment.

"Often in planning to photograph a significant war scene," writes Josephine Cobb of the National Archives, "the photographers found that no clear site could be discovered where their cameras could be set up, free of protruding branches or foliage. Occasionally a breath of wind, if not a stiff breeze, started up at the instant of exposure, thus ruining the chances of obtaining a picture. Horses, cows, and dogs, ambling back and forth within range of the camera, otherwise marked a failure for the photographer. . . .

"Once the views were made, there were other possibilities of failure: a bug on the wet collodion before the plate had dried; drops of perspiration settling on the plate within the darkroom tent; floating leaves and other debris in the creek or stream where the photographer washed his plates after their development. And the fact that only in strong sunlight could outdoor views be made at all, made the work of the Civil War photographers arduous and uncertain. . . ."

O'Sullivan's wagon had a storage and sleeping area in the front. There was a step in the rear, below the floor's level, to ease climbing aboard. A door was hung on the back to keep the light out. The jobs of coating, sensitizing, and developing the plates were done in cramped quarters in the rear. Wet-plate work usually had to be done within a few minutes, or the negative suffered loss of brilliancy and depth.

O'Sullivan was "civilian photographer" for the Army of the Potomac for three years, seeing action in many battles, from Second Manassas to Lee's surrender at Appomattox. Six Union generals came and went while he kept to his task. He recorded every aspect of war the technique of photography then permitted—the men and their officers, living and dead, camps, battlefields, ships, guns, railroads, bridges, wagon trains, the destruction of the land and the cities. For the first time the camera made it possible for people to see war as if they had witnessed it. This was how men lived and died in war. They saw it, and knew it was true.

In 1866 Gardner issued a two-volume *Photographic Sketch Book of the Civil War.* The one hundred pictures—forty-two of them O'Sullivan's—were seen at their best, for they were the actual positives pasted in place. (No facsimile, or reproduction, process had yet been invented to supplant the inferior woodcut adaptations of photos carried in the newspapers and magazines.)

A year later a United States government geologic mission set out to explore the Fortieth Parallel, the western wilderness between the front range of the Rocky Mountains and the eastern slope of the Sierra Nevada. The leader, Clarence King, selected O'Sullivan for the difficult pioneering task of staff photographer, no doubt because of his reputation as one of the most daring of the Civil War cameramen.

After three years in the mountains O'Sullivan was recruited for another trip, this time to the Isthmus of Darién (now the Isthmus of Panama) to see if it were suitable for a ship canal between the Atlantic and Pacific oceans. A year later O'Sullivan joined another expedition, led by Lieutenant George M. Wheeler, to make a series of surveys of the Southwest. He made three trips with Wheeler, in 1871, 1873, and 1875, photographing the deserts and mountains of Nevada, Arizona, Colorado, and New Mexico. The large cameras he used produced hundreds of superbly detailed photos that were published by the federal government in huge leather-bound volumes.

Now in his mid-thirties, O'Sullivan had shown repeatedly that magnificent documentary photographs could be taken under the most difficult and punishing conditions. Toward the end of 1875 he came back to quiet Staten Island and sank into obscurity. The scanty record shows that after his wife died suddenly he went to live with his father. In November, 1880, he was appointed photographer for the U. S. Treasury Department, where he worked briefly until tuberculosis forced him to resign. He died at West Brighton on Staten Island on January 14, 1882, leaving the enduring heritage of his portrait of war.

General Ulysses S. Grant holds council of war in Virginia, May 21, 1864. Grant is standing at left, leaning over shoulder of General George G. Meade, examining a map. Photo taken by O'Sullivan from church steeple.

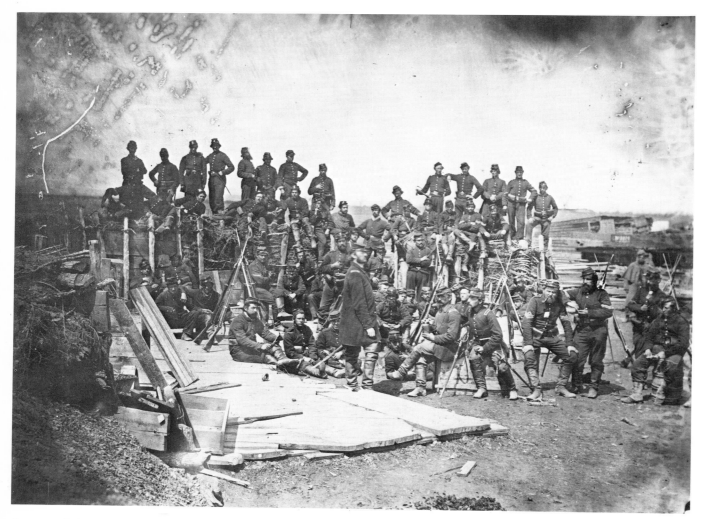

Company C, Forty-first New York Infantry,
after Second Battle of Bull Run, 1862.

*Telegraph Construction Corps of the Army of the
Potomac, putting up wire connecting
the Union Army with Washington, D. C.*

Slaves were liberated by the advancing Union troops or escaped from their masters by their own will. This family, with household goods piled on an oxcart, is crossing the Rappahannock River in August, 1862.

*Harvest of death in the Iron Brigade,
the Twenty-fourth Michigan Infantry, at Gettysburg.*

*Smoking ruins of a railroad bridge across the North Anne River
on the road to Richmond, Virginia, 1864.*

Union supply depot at Manassas Junction, Virginia, just after Confederate raiders had damaged rails and wrecked cars.

Dead Confederate sharpshooter, at foot of
Little Round Top, Gettysburg.

In fighting near Spotsylvania Courthouse, Virginia, on May 19, 1864, this Confederate soldier of Ewell's Corps was killed.

The end—recorded on a glass plate that broke.

JACOB A. RIIS

Jacob Riis was not a quiet one. He was so tough a fighter
that the New York City police force dreaded him. So did many
a mayor of the great city. Even landlords ran for cover when
they saw Jacob Riis coming.

It wasn't because he had an army behind him or because
he had any political power. He stood alone, much of the time,
and had only words—and pictures—as weapons.

But Jacob Riis's words, to take them first, weren't just
words. They were words that stood for facts, hard facts, facts
he gave his life to finding. And facts used properly, he always
said, would lead to action. He knew how to find them and
how to use them, for Jacob Riis was a newspaper reporter
—one of the greatest America has known. And one of the most
unusual, for he never wrote a sentence he didn't try to
substantiate.

On New York's East Side in the 1880s Riis saw thousands
of children working in the clothing factories for thirty cents
a day. Every one had a certificate saying he or she was fourteen
and therefore old enough to be employed. A recent Factory
Law had set that minimum age for workers. But it was clear
to Riis that many of the children were not even ten years of
age. When he asked the employers about it, they shrugged
and said, "Look at the certificates." He knew the certificates

31

were worthless, and since there was no birth registry in those days, he couldn't check in that way.

How could he prove that the children were too young to be slaving away in the factories? Sitting at home one night, he heard one of his own children crying. The baby was teething, and it hurt. Suddenly the idea came to him. He got a doctor to write out a table for him, showing at what age the various kinds of teeth usually appear in children.

Armed with the table, he marched back into the factories and pried open the little workers' mouths. Some of them objected. But he saw enough to give him proof. The child who did not yet have his canine teeth was certainly not fourteen, for those teeth should have been cut by age twelve at the latest. He showed that employers were forging work certificates and were breaking the child-labor law in great numbers.

That was only one of Riis's battles in the endless war against poverty and injustice. He fought every day to tear down the dilapidated tenements and to build new housing for their tenants; he fought for parks for the people walled up in the slums, for playgrounds for their children, for good teachers and decent schools.

Riis had enemies. They didn't like a reporter coming into their territory to expose unsavory practices they wanted to hide. Keeping things the way they were was usually profitable for them. Landlords made money out of jamming fifteen people into one or two rooms. Factory owners made money out of hiring children at lower wages than adults. Policemen and politicians kept their jobs longer if no one questioned how well these jobs were being done.

At first Riis's enemies tried to get rid of him by saying he didn't know what he was talking about. But that wasn't convincing. Jacob Riis not only saw what he was talking about —he had lived it himself.

It had started in 1870 when he came to America at the age
of twenty-one. He had been born in Denmark in 1849. His
father taught Latin and had a hard time raising a family of
fifteen on a teacher's small pay. He made a little extra money
by reporting for the local newspaper. Young Jacob didn't
want the long schooling his father had had. He preferred to
learn the carpenter's trade. At fifteen he was apprenticed to
a carpenter at home, and then he worked in Copenhagen for
several years to earn his trade certificate. At twenty-one he
proposed to a sixteen-year-old girl he had loved for years. But
her family didn't think a carpenter was good enough for her
and sent him away.

Riis decided the only way to forget her was to get as far
away as possible. With his small savings he bought passage to
America. When he stepped ashore in New York, the first thing
he did was to buy the biggest revolver he could find. He
strapped it outside his coat and paraded up Broadway, ready
for the buffaloes and Indians he'd read about. A policeman
stopped him and suggested he leave the revolver at home if he
didn't want it stolen.

Riis never fired the revolver, but it proved to be a lucky
investment. For the next seven years he wandered over the
strange country, living through the worst it had to offer. Every
time he was starving—and it was often—he would pawn the
revolver for a few dollars.

Homeless and lonely, he went from job to job, from city to
city. In the 1870s America suffered the worst depression it
had known to that time. Young Riis managed to live through it,
joining the jobless men who roved the city streets hunting
for work or a handout. Riis built huts for miners and mined coal
himself. He laid bricks and cut timber. He farmed and hunted
and trapped. He made bedsteads and harvested ice. He
sold furniture and peddled flatirons door to door. Many nights
he shivered in doorways. Sometimes he slept in police stations

where a filthy and stinking room was set aside for the many vagrants, the only provision the cities made for their homeless wanderers.

One day in New York City he saw a help wanted ad for a reporter on a weekly paper. Perhaps because his father in the old country had done some reporting, he thought he would try it, too. He got the job so easily he should have been suspicious. He worked hard for two weeks, but when he didn't get paid, he quit.

Half-starved, he hunted for work again. This time he got the job that began a new life. He became a reporter for a city news agency at ten dollars a week. It wasn't easy. He worked from ten one morning until two the next. But he stuck it out and learned the craft. His big chance came at age twenty-eight, when he landed a better job on the *New York Tribune,* one of the city's great papers. He was married now—to the same girl he had left in Denmark—and was raising a family.

When the *Tribune* reporter covering the police beat quit, Riis was given the assignment. He worked in a little office on Mulberry Street just across from Police Headquarters. Here he found his lifework. In 1888 he transferred to the *New York Evening Sun.*

The Dutchman, as other reporters called him, was laughed at in the beginning. But he couldn't be downed. He became the "boss reporter" on Mulberry Street, in the heart of New York's worst slums. The police reporter's job was to gather and handle all the news that meant trouble to someone—the murders, fires, suicides, and robberies—before the cases got into court. The police didn't cooperate, for they didn't like crimes to be publicized unless they had caught the criminal.

Riis didn't take reporting coolly. Behind the scenes he saw great human drama, the acts that meant grief, suffering, revenge, loss, pain. The alert reporter often had to turn detective himself to protect the public interest. One summer Riis's

curiosity while nosing around the Health Department led him
to think New York's water supply was being polluted at its
source upstate. Believing the city to be in danger of a deadly
cholera epidemic, he raced up to the Croton watershed and
traced every stream to its source. He found that many small
towns were pouring their sewage directly into New York City's
drinking water. His paper launched a crusade and forced the
city to buy land along the streams wide enough to guard
them against pollution. It cost millions of dollars, but it saved
countless lives.

Riis's greatest work was in making the public deeply aware
of living and working conditions on New York's Lower East
Side. To millions of immigrants this part of the city was the first
America they knew. Along its streets lived Italians, Slavs,
Jews from eastern Europe, Chinese, blacks up from the South,
Germans, and Irish. For years Riis walked the length of
Mulberry Street every morning between two and four o'clock,
seeing the East Side "when off its guard," he said. Its people
swarmed in thirty-seven thousand tenements no better than
pigsties, he found. Families lived in cellars, in crowded rooms
without windows or light; they slept in hallways, on fire
escapes, on roofs. They knew freezing cold in the winter and
burning heat in the summer. There was garbage, there
was noise, there were rats and lice, there were street fights
and gang warfare. And at the bottom of it all there was poverty,
poverty that bred disease and crime. The cost was enormous
in waste of human life. It was a cost paid by all of society.

Riis wrote day after day about the slums, exposing the
terrible conditions. But the people who did not like their
comfort disturbed called him a sensation-seeker. They said he
was making up much of it.

How could he convince them? Maybe drawings of what he
saw would do it—but he was no artist. He kept writing. It
seemed to make no impression. Then one day he read that two
men in Germany had developed a way to take pictures at

night or in dark places. It used a mixture called *blitzlichtpulver.* The mixture, invented in 1887, was magnesium powder, potassium chlorate, and antimony sulfide. When ignited, it gave a brilliant flash of light. At first it was made up in cartridges for use in a pistollike device. Riis was one of the first in America to try it. But the look of that weapon-gadget scared some of his photographic subjects into pulling out their own concealed weapons. So Riis tried putting the powder into a frying pan and igniting the mixture by hand. When it exploded, he would take his picture in the blinding flash and flee under cover of the thick smoke.

So again he invaded the slums, now with an ally in his fight to "let in the light where it was so much needed." He got his pictures—and there was no appeal from them. No landlord's defense could stand up against the camera's evidence. Unintentionally, Jacob Riis had become America's first journalist-photographer, and a pioneer in documentary photography.

Not content with newspaper reports, Riis took his pictures to the public in person. He made slides and told his story in churches and meeting halls. His photographs mirrored the horror of a city where almost half a million people—a third of the population—had to beg for food. A magazine editor went to one of his lectures and asked him to do an article. It was an instant sensation all over the country.

Better days began. Now a publisher asked him to do a book on the slums. He wrote every night, after returning from work. In 1890 the book, *How the Other Half Lives,* came out. It was a great success, even though it contained only nineteen line drawings based on his pictures and seventeen miserably printed halftones of his photographs. The technique of facsimile reproduction had not yet reached the point where photographs could be satisfactorily printed in newspapers or books.

So poor were the halftones that many years passed before
Riis was recognized as an important photographer as well
as a great reporter. In 1947 Alexander Alland made superb
enlargements from the fading images on a collection of
Riis's 4x5-inch glass plates he had found. Since that time the
pictures have been widely shown and reproduced. But it
was not until 1971 that an edition of *How the Other Half Lives*
appeared with thirty of the photographs from which the
original line drawings had come, plus seventy additional Riis
photographs related to the text.

Riis was always the reporter. As Lincoln Steffens, another
great reporter and reformer who knew him, said, "He not only
got the news—he cared about the news." He never rested.
He pushed and prodded, he coaxed and shouted, he showed
icy contempt or hot fury. He said he knew people tend to
be "as lazy as things will let them be. It takes a lot of telling
to make a city know when it is doing wrong." However, he
added, "That was what I was there for."

Riis's photographs, combined with the work of his pen, had a
powerful influence. Technically his images were flawed. In
composition his work fell short of that produced by the
documentary photographers whose way he paved. He was
not concerned with art. "Yet his pictures," wrote the critic A. D.
Coleman, "remain vital and urgent, transcending even their
undeniable importance as records; they teem with the same
life as did the streets and apartments where they were made,
and they are sensitive to the tragedies of oppressed people's
lives. . . . Present-day concerned photographers owe a debt
to Riis."

So did the people whose lives he labored to make better.
His unrelenting struggle wiped out the horror of Mulberry
Bend, brought light to dark hallways, cleaner water to tenement
taps, desks to schoolrooms, settlement houses to slums,
and improved conditions to factories. The camera was only

the tool a humane man needed to express the misery and squalor he found in the slums. But from the depth of his feelings came great pictures that, by both informing and moving others, helped start a revolt against urban rot.

The Mulberry Bend, about 1888–89.

Bandits' Roost,
at 39½ Mulberry Street.

Police station lodgers, Elizabeth Street.

*Ready for the Sabbath Eve
in a coal cellar, Ludlow Street.*

Sweatshop in a Ludlow Street tenement.

A class in the condemned Essex Market School.

He slept in this cellar for four years.

Homeless boys in sleeping quarters, Mulberry Street.

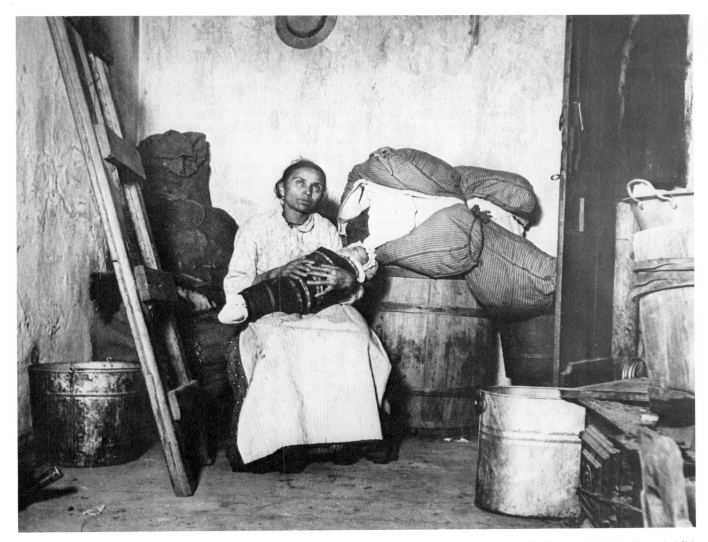

*Italian ragpicker's wife and child,
at home on Jersey Street.*

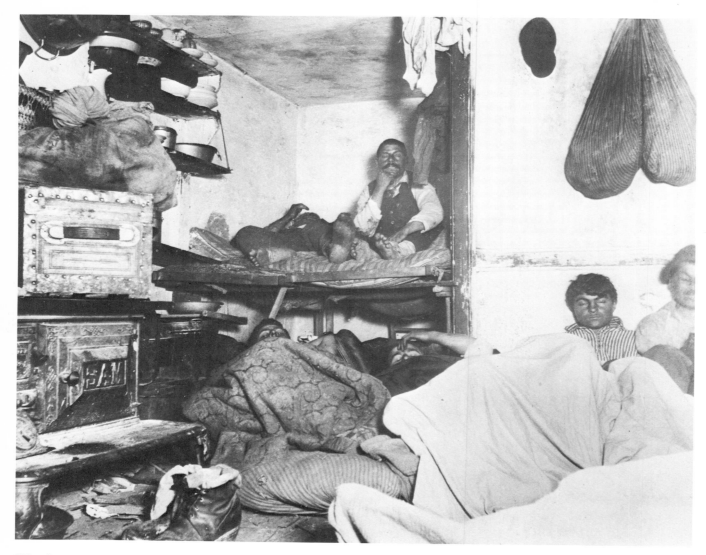

"Five Cents a Spot"—
lodgers in a Bayard Street tenement.

LEWIS W. HINE

The first time he did it was the hardest. (He would do it again, many times, but he would always be scared.) The sun had been up only a few minutes. The Carolina sky was streaked a pale green. The last few children scrambled through the gate just before it banged shut, then raced on skinny legs for the door. They looked like wisps of cut grass blown before the wind. At the door the guard demanded to know who he was and what he wanted. He stood with his left side turned away from the guard, the lunch pail dangling from his hand. Small as it was, the pail felt like a chunk of granite with the Graflex hidden at the bottom. He was the fire inspector, he told the guard. He wanted to make the rounds of the mill to check the equipment. The guard grunted, said nothing about seeing identification, and kicked the door open.

Inside, the air was warm, moist, swimming with lint. The workers stood before the spinning frames. He noticed some of the frames had shorter legs to suit the size of the children. He climbed the stairs, up one flight, then another, till he was on the top floor. Nobody in the vast open space seemed to notice him. Down the long rows the children were intent on their work. As he passed, only one or two glanced up.

At the far end of the room he saw a corner almost cut off from view by a pile of packing cases. He headed for it and found a girl he thought was about fourteen years old at work. He took a box, put it in a darker corner, and sat on it. The girl looked up in a few minutes when he didn't move off. He glanced around nervously and then, in a low, gentle voice, told the girl to keep working and not look up while he talked. He said he was there to find out what children did in the cotton mills, what their hours and wages and working conditions were. He talked straight and simply. The people I am working with are your friends, he said. They want the facts, to tell the country about the children who work. They want to get laws passed to make life better for all of you.

There was something so earnest and direct about him that she must have felt she could trust the stranger. Yet her back was stiff under the ragged dress as he talked. She kept her fingers flying. When he stopped, there was an agonizingly long silence. Then, turning her head to the side and down, she began to talk. She was only ten, he discovered, not fourteen. She had a brother of five and a sister of six working in the same mill. They all worked twelve hours each day. If they got sick and left the mill, they lost the day's pay. If they stayed home, company men rode to their doors and hounded them out of bed back to the loom. Sometimes she worked on the night shift—all night long. When she got home, she was usually too tired to take off her clothes before crawling into bed. For the day shift she got up at 4:45 in the morning when the mill whistle shrieked and with her family gulped down a handful of food and hurried off to work. Yes, her mother and father worked in the mill, too. Everyone in the family did. There had been two other children between her and the five and six year olds. Both of them had died a few years after starting to work.

As she talked, he had taken out a small pad, and holding it on his knee with one hand covering it, he'd scribbled notes with the other. When she stopped, after answering most of his questions, he whispered to her to keep on working. He reached

down into the lunch pail for his camera, and leaning against
a wall in shadow, he swiftly took her picture. Then he shot
another down the length of the long room, catching the whole
row of children in his viewer. Hastily he shoved the camera
out of sight again and prepared to leave. As he passed the girl,
he reached out and pressed her shoulder lightly. The bones
were like a small bird's under his hand. He walked quietly
back down the room, pausing now and then as though to
examine the fire equipment, making scratches on his pad. A
foreman passed and nodded to him. Soon he was down the
steps, through the door, then across the yard to the gate, and
outside he was safe at last.

It was the year 1909 when Lewis W. Hine smuggled his
camera into the southern textile mills. Paul Strand, one of
America's great photographers, who studied with Hine in 1908,
has underscored the courage it took in those early years to
photograph child labor in the South. It was like entering the
enemy's armed camp, he said. Hine risked the threats of
foremen and factory owners who feared what his camera might
expose. They were right to be afraid: the pictures and stories
he brought away with him shocked the nation and prepared it
to support remedial legislation.

Apparently Hine did not always have to take his pictures
secretly, for some of his prints show foremen standing by,
sometimes smiling into the camera. Such men may not yet
have learned what trouble photographs could make for their
employers. Or perhaps they were so flattered to be asked to
pose that they forgot to think about the possible consequences.
Today, of course, few are so naive.

Although many were made under bad conditions, almost all
of Hine's photographs were remarkably powerful. The deep
sympathy he felt for the child workers always came through.
The pictures and information he gathered became weapons in
the hands of the National Child Labor Committee. The photos

were seen everywhere—in posters, in books and pamphlets, in newspapers and magazines. They were dramatic proof of the tragedy of child labor to which America had been blind.

The man who made America see the truth started out not as a photographer but as a laborer. Hine was born in Oshkosh, Wisconsin, in 1874. He worked at many unskilled jobs until he decided to get more education. He took courses at night school, and then went to the Oshkosh Normal School, where teachers were trained. The principal, Frank Manny, liked Hine and urged him on.

Encouraged, Hine went to the University of Chicago. The city of Chicago was then the center of a reform movement. The trade unions, the university professors, the welfare workers like Jane Addams, were all talking about and working for a new and better America. They were sickened by the waste and inhumanity created by the swift industrial growth in the years since the Civil War. They wanted an America that put equality and freedom before profits. The welfare of the people should be the concern of the government, they said, not the welfare of corporations.

Hine was excited by the new ideas around him. When his friend and teacher Frank Manny was appointed principal of the Ethical Culture School in New York, Hine, too, left Chicago. He took a job teaching science in Manny's school.

It was there that his life took another turn. Manny began to experiment with photography as a way of making school activities more meaningful. He chose Hine to become school photographer. Knowing nothing about the craft, Hine taught himself simply by using the camera.

It was 1903. Cameras and film had been developed to the point where men with hand cameras were setting the standard. Amateurs were often doing better work than the professionals. They showed more imagination, took more chances, dared to break the rules. Already, one amateur, Jacob Riis, had startled the country with his great photos of slum life in New York.

By 1905 Hine had learned enough camera technique to try a major work. He turned to Ellis Island, the place in New York harbor where every day thousands of immigrants landed from Europe. They came to the promised land looking for decent jobs and the freedom they had not known in the old country.

Ellis Island was packed with lonely people, eager to taste American life, but frightened by the unknown. Hine's camera caught the trust and hope in the immigrants' faces and made a vivid record of the newcomers that is now a national treasure.

The way Hine worked on that first major task became his standard. When he started, he used a 5x7 view camera, magnesium powder for open flash, and glass plates. Later he added a 4x5 Graflex. His equipment was simple; so was his method. With it he moved directly to the truth.

By now he knew photography would be his lifework. In 1908 he published an article about attempts to improve the life of the poor in New York. His pictures showed the filth and disease of the slums. The editor of a magazine devoted to social reform saw the piece and asked Hine to join the staff of *The Survey* as photographer. Hine gave up his teaching job and from that day on used his camera to reform social conditions.

His first assignment was to picture the life of immigrant workers in the Pittsburgh steel district. Then he photographed the workers building the New York State Barge Canal. From that he went to investigating the rapidly growing slums of Chicago and Washington, D. C.

It was while studying the life of the poor that Hine learned how poverty ruined childhood. In the streets and alleys of the slums he saw children robbed of their futures, their bodies stunted and their minds twisted. He learned of children as young as five made to do harsh, cheap labor in the factories.

Already reformers had begun to fight this crime against childhood. The National Child Labor Committee (NCLC) was campaigning for laws to protect children. When the committee head saw Hine's work in *The Survey,* he asked Hine to become staff investigator and photographer.

Hine took the job in 1908 and gave all his heart and strength to it. By that time over 1.7 million children under fifteen years of age were working in fields, factories, mines, and sweatshops. But such figures were just units in a census report. No one could call up in imagination's eye the meaning of that fact—1.7 million child wage earners. Lewis Hine knew how to make the figure flesh and blood. "Photographs of revelation," one editor called them.

Hine was always on the move with his camera; now in a Georgia cotton mill, now in a Pennsylvania coal mine, now in a New York sweatshop. He went into the homes of working children, the slum tenements, and the rural shacks. He asked the children their names, measured their heights against his coat buttons, jotted down their ages. He went from anger to despair as he saw no end to the tasks the industrial age was setting for child labor. "Tasks?" he asked once in bitter irony. "Not so—they are 'opportunities' for the child and the family to enlist in the service of industry and humanity. In unselfish devotion to their homework vocation, they relieve the over-burdened manufacturer, help him pay his rent, supply his equipment, take care of his rush and slack seasons, and help him to keep down his wage scale. Of course they must accept with cheery optimism the steady decline in wages that inevitably follows in the wake of homework. Isn't it better for everyone to be working instead of expecting father to do it all?"

His photographs marched thousands of children out of the mines and factories and paraded them before the nation's eyes. The comfortable and easy could see what working twelve hours a day or a night at miserable wages did to children. They could see the tired young eyes, the blank faces, the gray skin, the crippled hands, the broken bodies. "The great social peril is darkness and ignorance," Hine said. "Light is required. Light! Light in floods!"

Hine's photographs became the core of pamphlets, bulletins, newspaper and magazine articles, and books, all exposing and attacking child labor. He did not insist on quality of reproduction if he could gain immediacy of effect. At least a score of the NCLC pamphlets were shaped from information he gathered in his reports to the committee. Some he wrote in full or in part, in addition to supplying the photos. Costing a nickel or a dime, the pamphlets were distributed nationally. Hine often spoke at NCLC conferences and showed his pictures through stereopticon enlargements. His biographer, Judith M. Gutman, says he took five thousand photographs for the committee; some five hundred of them have been published.

Hine's role was summed up by the committee's chairman, Owen R. Lovejoy: "The work Hine did for this reform was more responsible than all other efforts in bringing the need to public attention. The evils were intellectually but not emotionally recognized until his skill, vision, and artistic finesse focused the camera intelligently on these social problems."

Hine did work for the committee well into the 1930s. It was a long hard fight, against the opposition of employers, to change things. Not until 1938 did a federal law pass against child labor that the Supreme Court let stand.

At the end of the First World War Hine went to Europe for the Red Cross, to record its work in helping war victims. During this assignment he began using film for the first time, as well as glass plates. Then he wandered through southeastern Europe, photographing the effects of war and disease upon the people of the Balkans.

When he came back to the United States, he decided to show another side of the workingman's life. His camera had exposed bad working conditions. The machines of industry could hurt people, if uncontrolled. But workers could still take pride in what they made. The machine did not destroy man's dignity, he believed. Hine took his camera into power-houses, factories, docks, railroad yards, and truck terminals, recording the skills of workers and the pleasure taken in a job worth doing. It was his pictures, never less important than the words of a writer about the subject, that led someone to invent the phrase "photo story" to describe such work. His only book, *Men at Work,* published in 1932, was a beautiful tribute to labor and is considered a pioneer in the picture book form.

Hine's greatest pictures in this book came out of the construction of the Empire State Building. In 1931 he was hired to photograph it stage by stage. From digging the hole in the ground to putting the last rivet on the mooring mast, Hine covered its growth. He climbed floor by floor with the workers as they built the world's tallest structure, carrying his view camera and his tripod on his shoulder. He was in his late fifties by then. But he seemed never to tire.

There were many other jobs to do in that decade of the New Deal. He also photographed several of the exciting experiments of the federal government—the rural nursing project, the youth training program, the work relief and the farm electrification projects. He was busy on one of these assignments when he died on November 3, 1940, after a brief illness.

What Hine had been doing for nearly thirty years, almost alone, laid the foundation for the new school of "concerned photography." Ben Shahn, one of the superb team of photographers working in the 1930s for the Farm Security Administration unit, said, "Hine was one of the great. I don't know a photographer who has not been conscious of, and influenced to some extent by, Lewis Hine."

Critic A. D. Coleman believes that "Hine's way of seeing has had an incalculable effect upon the vision of all subsequent documentarians, and thus has in a certain way dictated our own view of the world.''

Hine had begun as a teacher, and he never really left teaching. ''There are two things I wanted to do,'' he said. ''I wanted to show the things that had to be corrected. I wanted to show the things that had to be appreciated.'' All his pictures are a record of the truth the way he saw it, the truth he wanted other people to see. In 1920 he was given one-man shows in New York by the Civic Art Club and the National Arts Club —the first photographer to be exhibited by artists. His pictures were works of art—and at the same time tools for helping people to make their lives richer and better.

''The residual power of these pictures,'' wrote the critic Alan Trachtenberg, ''is not simple to explain. In part it lies in their directness. The visual fact, captured often under extremely difficult and hazardous circumstances, is rarely editorialized by tricks of lighting or staging. Hine adopted the camera's rigor as his own, a rigor that extends to his exact notations of data—place, names, age—with each exposure. His refusal to sentimentalize lends force to his compassion. We feel that each image has been elicited by an intense engagement, a disciplined love: a love that wishes simultaneously to heal as it reveals.''

Spinner in cotton mill, Augusta, Georgia, 1909.

Mill girl, South Carolina, 1908.

*Sweeper and doffer boys in Lancaster mill,
South Carolina, 1908.*

*"Little Fattie," six-year-old newsboy,
St. Louis, Missouri, 1910.*

Newsboy, New York City, 1910.

Mortaria family making flower wreaths,
New York City, 1912.

Making garments in a New York tenement, 1910.

Coal mine worker, Pennsylvania, 1911.

Coal mine workers, Pennsylvania, 1911

Breaker boys in coal mine, Pennsylvania, 1911.

DOROTHEA LANGE

Thieves' highway" they called it, and twice a week after
school Dorothea Lange had to walk it alone to reach the library
on the Lower East Side where her mother worked. The Bowery
was full of petty thieves and their allies, the fences who
received stolen goods. Dorothea walked block after block,
stepping across the bodies of drunks sprawled on the
pavement. Already, at the age of twelve, she knew how to keep
her face impassive so that she would draw no attention.
That self-protective, expressionless face she would use her
whole life in photographing people in strange places. "I can turn
it on and off," she said once. "If I don't want anybody to see
me, I can make the kind of face so eyes will go off me."

Hard as the Bowery trip was, it was part of the preparation
for the work she would give her life to. Now she crossed
Chatham Square where two elevated railways clattered over
the tangled confluence of streets. Having arrived at the branch
library, she would sit reading till her mother's shift was over.
The room's windows looked out onto the tenements of the Tenth
Ward—Jewtown, as Jacob Riis called it in these years. Over
three hundred thousand people, immigrants from eastern and
southern Europe, were packed into a square mile here. The
five-story tenements were rank with dirt and disease; the alleys,
hallways, and cellars crowded with children playing among
trash and tramps. From her library window Dorothea could

look straight into the life of those teeming tenements whose brick walls stretched up both sides of the street. She could see whole families laboring, sewing garments at sweatshop rates for contractors. "I looked into all these lives," she said, "lives of a tradition completely alien to me, but I watched."

Dorothea Lange still lived in Hoboken, New Jersey, where she had been born on May 26, 1895. But when her mother got a job as librarian on the East Side, she took Dorothea across the Hudson into New York every day, and left her at P. S. 62 before going to work. For two years, through the seventh and eighth grades, Dorothea went to that ghetto school, the only Gentile, as she recalled it, among three thousand Jewish children. She learned what it was to be in a minority. She was an outsider among children hungry for knowledge and fighting their way up out of the slums. Amid such overwhelming ambition, she felt lost. She couldn't keep up. There was no social life in that school, so her afternoons were spent at her mother's library, reading. She remembered "looking and looking and looking" at pictures. She loved all kinds, not only photographs.

Dorothea's grandparents had come from Germany as immigrants. Several of her uncles became lithographers. It may have been from them that she early absorbed a feeling for what was pure and what was corrupt in workmanship. Mr. Lange left his family while Dorothea was young, and her mother had to support the family on fifty-five dollars a month.

From the windows of her New Jersey home Dorothea could see the Hackensack Meadows, dotted with red brick buildings, crossed by wooden fences, and laced with clotheslines strung across backyards. "It's beautiful," she said once, and when an aunt snorted, "To you, everything is beautiful!" she was startled. She hadn't realized till then that she saw things that way.

Finishing at P. S. 62, Dorothea went uptown to Wadleigh High School. She was no longer a minority of one, but the school was for girls only, and she was miserable. She often skipped classes, walking from above One Hundredth Street way down to the Battery at the foot of Manhattan. She came to know city life walking these crowded streets, and learned not to be afraid when alone. All parts of the world, she began to feel, were her natural element. Her mother didn't know what she was doing on the loose. "I wasn't being taken care of," she said years later. "I was neglected, thank God!" The independence she was trying out put iron in her.

What added to her strength, strangely, was a physical weakness she was born with. She was lame. "I think it was perhaps the most important thing that happened to me," she said, looking back from her mid-sixties. "It formed me, guided me, instructed me, helped me, and humiliated me. All these things at once. I've never gotten over it, and I am aware of the force and the power of it. My lameness as a child and my acceptance, finally, of my lameness truly opened gates for me."

One day, when she was about seventeen, Dorothea said to her mother, "I want to be a photographer."

"You have to have something to fall back on," Mrs. Lange replied—not surprisingly, for her daughter had no camera and had never taken a picture. And who knew if you could make a living with a camera?

But Dorothea didn't want security. She knew, she said, "it was dangerous to have something to fall back on."

The family insisted she get training for some occupation that would always give her a livelihood. Her mother had no money, but relatives put up enough for her to enroll at the New York Training School for Teachers.

Mrs. Lange was working now in the juvenile courts of Jersey City, and Dorothea was living with her, a brother, and an aunt. She attended class, but her mind was elsewhere. She got a camera and gave every spare moment to working with it.

"I've never not been sure that I was a photographer," she once said, "any more than you would not be sure you were yourself! I was a photographer, getting to be a photographer, or wanting to be a photographer, or beginning—but some phase of photographer I've always been."

A year later she looked for professional help. She visited Arnold Genthe's studio on Fifth Avenue. Genthe had become celebrated through his pictures of life in San Francisco's Chinatown and of the devastation caused that city by the great earthquake and fire of 1906. Now in his mid-forties, he was one of New York's most prominent photographers, specializing in portraits of theater and film stars. He took Dorothea on as one of his assistants, paying her fifteen dollars a week to work afternoons and evenings. His was a limited technique, she thought, shooting under a battery of lights with tightly controlled conditions. It was a good commercial formula that made money. She believed in Genthe's sense of beauty. He was doing what he wanted to do, and loved it. But twenty-year-old Dorothea knew it was not for her. What she learned from Genthe was a good deal about portrait photography as a trade.

Her next job, for twelve dollars a week, was with the studio of Spencer-Beatty, a woman who did not take pictures herself but hired camera operators. Before Dorothea was really prepared, she was assigned to substitute for an absent photographer and took the big 8x10 camera out alone to shoot the wealthy Brokaw family. She had learned how professionals behaved on the job and what people wanted from a studio portrait. The results pleased the Brokaws. Her next assignment was to photograph Sir Herbert Beerbohm-Tree, who was starring in the role of Cardinal Richelieu. He liked her and made the job easy. Now she could call herself a portrait photographer.

There would be four or five other photographers she would learn much from in one way or another. "Lovable old hacks," she called some of them. What one of them said to her once she echoed years later when young hopefuls brought her their portfolios. "You don't know how important it is to have a good negative," she said. And she sometimes added, "What you have in your negative is transmitted to your print, and if you have to do a lot of things in between, wouldn't it be much better to make the negative good in the first place?"

From some of the men and women to whom she apprenticed herself, she learned things in reverse—how not to do this or that. She was a sponge, soaking up whatever seemed useful, no matter where it came from. She "stumbled" into most of what she learned, but, she said, "I must have been going after it all the time or it wouldn't have come to me."

In 1917, on Genthe's advice, she signed up for a seminar in photography given by Clarence H. White at Columbia University. White was one of the "purist" group, photographers who did not try to imitate the work of painters. Lange thought he had a fine sense of the human figure; his work was luminous; he used the camera as a natural instrument, the way a musician played the flute.

In that small group Lange was the one who never did the assignments and never brought in work for White to judge. She was just there. White was a hesitant, fumbling talker. She could not remember anything he said, except that he never was negative. "He gave everyone some feeling of encouragement in some peculiar way." Technique, shortcuts, manipulations, how it's done—he was silent on all that. He was a man of great tenderness, she said, who knew when something was beautiful and could photograph it that way. In him she sensed a kind of "unconscious, instinctive, photographic life." He had an uncanny gift for touching the lives of his students.

During these years Lange had rented a chicken coop on the Jersey Palisades to use as her darkroom. She now had a big camera and two lenses, and night and day she worked at learning darkroom techniques. She experienced the "darkroom terrors," and this never left her. "It still is a gambler's game, photography," she said, noting that you have to have a streak of gambler in you, unless you work within a formula. She enjoyed the process of making something. "I like doing things where when you're finished, there's something that's there, that exists." None of her pictures from this early period survive. They were stored in boxes at her mother's, and after moving several times Mrs. Lange threw them out.

What was it that formed the young photographer? Not so much events that happened to her, she said, as persons. A Genthe or a White, certainly, but others, too, who lived a different kind of life. Isadora Duncan was one. Lange saw her dance at the Metropolitan Opera House in New York. It was not as a theatrical performance that it mattered so much to the young woman, "but as an extension of human possibility." Isadora Duncan was one of the people from whom she learned what *quality* meant.

Emily Sanderfield was another of those rare people—a nurse who related to her as an adopted aunt. Troubled and lonely as a child, Lange sensed a calm in the starchly uniformed woman who seemed to live her whole life within a hospital. When she talked with Emily in her cell-like room, Lange perceived in her a feeling of serenity, of a healing inner peace she felt could come only from complete self-abnegation.

By 1918 Lange thought that with her camera she could probably earn a living wherever she chose to go. Her technique was uncertain, but not her direction. And she had print sense, which some people never acquire. She left New York and found a job as a photofinisher in a camera supply house in San Francisco. She joined a camera club on Market Street for its darkroom privileges. A year later, helped by a friend, she opened her own portrait studio on Sutter Street. It was a success at once. Not because she was doing anything phenomenal; she was not trying to be a *great* photographer. "I just did everything I could to make it as good as I could. And good meant to me being careful, filling a need, really pleasing the people for whom I was working." And that, she added, did not mean pandering to their vanity, but being honest and truthful. "I tried, with every person I photographed, to reveal them as closely as I could." Thirty years later, people could still remember portraits of hers from this early period.

In 1920 she married the painter Maynard Dixon. They had two sons in a marriage that lasted fifteen years. In 1929, when the stock market crash signaled the coming of the Great Depression, her studio was on Montgomery Street, at the crossroads of Chinatown and the Barbary Coast, close by the wholesale market district. This depression, the worst the country had yet suffered, came on hard and fast, engulfing millions. It would last all through the 1930s, though no one knew it then.

Within two months several million people were thrown out of work. Many businesses came to a dead stop. Salesmen were fired, factories cut down on production, construction was halted, banks tightened up on credit. The wheels slowed, then stopped. Pink slips—the boss's notice that you were fired—appeared in millions more pay envelopes.

From her window on a corner of Montgomery Street, Dorothea Lange watched the flow of life. "The unemployed would drift by, would stop, and I could just see that they did not know where next," she recalled. "The studio room was one flight up and I looked down as long as I could, and then one day I said to myself, 'I'd better make this happen,' and that started me."

She shot what she saw and put a print on the wall. Her customers looked and said, "Yes, but what are you going to do with it?"

She had no idea. She was simply compelled to respond

with her camera to what was around her. She felt controlled by the life that beat in upon her. There were more such candid pictures, different from what she had been doing for years —photographing people out of their natural milieu, in the synthetic setting of a studio. She had also tried to photograph outdoors the natural forms she liked—pine trees, a stump, the way sunlight came through the big-leaved skunk cabbage, showing all its veins. "But I just couldn't do it," she said. She was discovering that photographing people in the context of their lives, people whose lives touched her somehow, was her way, and no other.

And leaving the studio to go out on the city's streets, she found her commitment—to people. At this moment in American history it was the people a collapsing economic system had tossed on the garbage dump. "White Angel Breadline, San Francisco, 1933," the photograph of an unshaven man leaning over a railing, holding an empty tin can, his back to the crowd waiting for a handout, sucked the viewer into the whirlpool of the depression. It was the first picture representative of her new work to become widely known. It is still one of the most moving images of what happened to Americans in the thirties.

It was now that she remembered her childhood wanderings in New York's Bowery. Here, too, she wasn't one of the unemployed herself, but she had to move among the tormented men and women—the angry and the sullen—with her camera. She was fearful at first, but she learned how to do it, and soon saw that people would trust her. On May Day, 1933, she photographed the unemployed demonstration at the San Francisco Civic Center and the year after that the city's great longshoremen's strike. She did not think of exhibiting the pictures when she gave herself these assignments. She was still taking portraits to help support her family. More and more, however, she wanted to devote herself completely to this new work.

In 1935 she got her chance. It happened indirectly through Willard Van Dyke, the photographer, who had seen her new pictures and had exhibited them in his Oakland studio in 1934. Dr. Paul Taylor, an economics professor at the University of California in nearby Berkeley, saw the show and secured one of her photos as the frontispiece to his article in the *Survey Graphic* on the San Francisco general strike. He met Lange for the first time when Van Dyke arranged an expedition to a sawmill run by a commune, one of the many that sprang up in the early depression years, hoping to survive by barter and self-help. She photographed the group, "but not well," she said, because she didn't yet know enough to do it right. Still, Van Dyke wrote a perceptive article about her pictures for *Camera Craft,* anticipating remarkably the great photographer she would become.

Lange went on field trips with teams led by Taylor, who was director of a state relief project trying to rehabilitate farmers hit by the depression. Dispossessed sharecroppers and tenant farmers whose leases had not been renewed had taken to the road, joining the nation's harvest hands and migrant workers. They were following the seasonal crops as pickers and laborers, averaging little more than a hundred dollars a year.

Taylor's team had no provision for paying a photographer, so Lange was listed as a typist. In April, 1935, great dust storms followed a terrible drought, denuding the plains. The desperate farmers of Oklahoma and Texas fled into California. So sudden and huge was the influx that the panicky state almost closed its border to the refugees. Lange was the first to photograph the new migrants, as later John Steinbeck would be the first major novelist to write about them in his *Grapes of Wrath.*

In December, 1935, Lange married Taylor and moved from San Francisco to Berkeley. The two of them continued working together, and it was from him that Lange learned how to be a good social observer. She acquired the discipline needed to handle assignments in the field that could last for weeks or months or had directives that might be too broad or vague.

Was it hard for her to do? "Everything is difficult to photograph well," she said once. But it's easier when you get involved in what you're doing. It wasn't only photographing the conditions of farm labor, but going behind the conditions to put them in their right perspective. She watched Taylor talk to the migrant workers and saw how a good social scientist could get answers to questions without making people feel self-conscious or embarrassed. She realized that most people are eager to talk about themselves and their own experiences when approached the right way.

Their collaboration—the first of a social scientist and a photographer—produced effective reports that led to practical results. California built camps to shelter the migrants decently. Even more far-reaching, the work of the Lange-Taylor team anticipated the move by the federal government to include a photographic unit in the agency that later came to be known as the Farm Security Administration. Roy Stryker, an engineer and economist brought from Columbia University to prepare a history of the government's farm resettlement program, saw a portfolio of Lange's California photos. The stark images of the migratory workers had a powerful impact. This was the way for the FSA to report what was happening, he decided.

Lange and other photographers joined the FSA unit. Among them were such people as Walker Evans, Ben Shahn, Russell Lee, Marion Post Wolcott, John Vachon, Arthur Rothstein, and Carl Mydans. In the next four years Lange did most of her best-known work. She had found what she had to do and the place to do it.

Sometimes she worked with other people, sometimes alone. Part of her job in the field was to get notes on the people she photographed and the conditions of their lives. Usually she didn't read up on her subject before going out, but did so while on the job. The most fruitful research, however, came after she had returned from the field. She preferred to follow her instincts, rather than let study influence her beforehand. That way she might discover what had been neglected or unknown. She tried to open herself as wide as she could, to be herself, "like a piece of unexposed, sensitized material. . . . To know ahead what you're looking for means you're only photographing your own preconceptions, which is very limiting and often false."

In her FSA service Lange learned not to rely on past performances, not to linger in comfortable ruts, not to shy away from strange depths. She had to work in painful heat and cold, in storms of sand and wind. "What am I doing here?" she sometimes asked herself. "What drives me to do this hard thing?" The end of a working day was always a great relief. But at the moment when she was doing her job, when she thought, "Maybe that was all right, maybe that will be it," she knew the greatest satisfaction. What she was doing, wrote author and critic George P. Elliott, "was picturing some of the disgracefully invisible people of our society, making them visible to all with humane eyes to see."

Her pictures, like those of others on the FSA team who would become legends in their own time, *persuaded.* They were seen everywhere—in newspapers, magazines, exhibitions. They made Americans know how unbalanced, how unfair, how wrong, how unjust, their society had become. Edward Steichen, one of the master photographers of the century, called the FSA photographs "the most remarkable human documents ever rendered in pictures." They were photographs, another critic said, that "altered America." As the depression decade came to an end, Pare Lorentz noted in *U.S. Camera 1941* that "if there are transient camps, and better working conditions, and a permanent agency seeking to help migratory workers, Lange . . . and Steinbeck . . . have done more for these tragic nomads than all the politicians of the country."

Perhaps Lange put it best herself. What she was trying
to do, she said, was "to say something about the despised, the
defeated, the alienated . . . about the crippled, the helpless,
the rootless . . . about duress and trouble . . . about the last
ditch."

American photojournalism was born in these years of
the thirties. *Life* magazine appeared late in 1936, and soon
was joined by *Look, Photo, Friday, Picture, Click,* and many
others. They were both an outlet for pictorial reporting and a
stimulus. Popular awareness of the power of the visual image
was kindled. And millions of amateurs with camera in hand
began to watch the world more closely.

Photojournalism developed rapidly because it could be
marketed to the mass-circulation magazines and newspapers.
The problem of reproducing photos, which had made the
work of Timothy O'Sullivan and Jacob Riis visible chiefly in
woodcuts, had been solved through the halftone printing
process.

But documentary photography, as Dorothea Lange viewed
it, developed slowly. Good examples were scarce, she said.
"Mostly it's something people love to *talk* about and very few
do." Why? Because it's hard to do, and it usually pays poorly.
People don't demand it. Photojournalism, on the other hand,
is quicker and easier to do. It can be superb, she said, but
it's not the same as documentary, that kind of picture taking
"where you go in over your head, not just up to your neck."

To her the documentary photograph was not simply a
factual photograph. Rather it was a picture that carried "the
full meaning of the episode or the circumstance or the situation
. . . that can only be revealed by a quality the artist responds
to." The documentary photographer and the artist—to Dorothea
Lange there was no warfare between them. They were one.

She did not define the "quality" she spoke of. Perhaps Roy
Stryker came near to what she meant when he wrote:

"Documentary is an approach, not a technic; an affirmation, not a negation. . . . The documentary attitude is not a denial of the plastic elements which must remain essential criteria in any work. It merely gives these elements limitation and direction. Thus composition becomes emphasis, and line sharpness, focus, filtering, mood—all those components included in the dreamy vagueness 'quality'—are made to serve an end: to speak, as eloquently as possible, of the thing to be said in the language of pictures. . . . The question is not what to picture nor what camera to use. Every phase of our time and our surroundings has vital significance and any camera in good repair is an adequate instrument. The job is to know enough about the subject matter to find its significance in itself, and in relation to its surroundings, its time, and its function."

In the winter of 1938–39 Dorothea Lange and Paul Taylor worked on a book called *An American Exodus: A Record of Human Erosion,* which became a classic example of how the documentary image can be wedded to the printed word. Its form emerged from their team effort to make people understand "easily, clearly, and vividly" the exodus from the soil of millions of Americans during the depression decade. They set their theme upon a tripod of photographs, captions, and text. Printed with the pictures were excerpts from talk heard when the photographs were being taken. The reader knows what the people in the photos think, not what the authors guessed might be their unspoken thoughts. The book was published at the end of 1939.

During the next few years Lange took occasional assignments from government agencies other than the FSA. When war with Japan came in December, 1941, over one hundred thousand Japanese-Americans living on the Pacific Coast were forced into internment camps, deprived of their constitutional rights as well as their property. The effect of that collapse in national conscience was photographed by Dorothea Lange on assignment from the War Relocation Authority. Her pictures are documents of the survival of human dignity under the crushing weight of a brutal system. It is ironic that the very authority that carried out the racist policy commissioned the photographs that will never let us forget this national sin.

In the next two years Lange did work for the Office of War Information, but none of these negatives remain. They were lost in shipment. Her last work before a long period of illness was to photograph the United Nations founding conference in San Francisco in the spring of 1945. When some of her strength returned five years later, she began to work in many scattered places of the world—Utah, Ireland, California, Asia, Latin America, Egypt. While working abroad with her husband in these years, she suffered great physical pain. Nevertheless, she produced some of her best photographs.

In 1964 it was discovered she had cancer. "Just when I have gotten on the track," she said, "I find that I am going to die. There are so many things I have yet to do that it would take several lifetimes in which to do them all. It's hell to get sick." She spent her last year assembling a retrospective show of her life's work. She died on October 11, 1965. Three months later the exhibit opened at the Museum of Modern Art in New York City.

"Truly great art such as Dorothea Lange's," wrote the critic Allan Temko, "belongs so completely to its own time that it transcends time, and belongs to all civilization to come. The underlying principle of classic art of course is not simply permanence, for many worthless things are relatively long-lasting. Its main principle is intrinsic excellence. And such excellence rests not on technique, although every great artist is necessarily a great technician—and Dorothea was one of the finest. Such excellence is the resultant of spiritual and intellectual insight which leads the artists to discover—where others do not seek even to find—new truths in the cause of man."

Tractored out, Childress County, Texas, 1938.

These farm implements should never have been used,
for they destroyed a naturally rich grazing area.
Mills, New Mexico, May, 1935.

Migratory laborer's wife,
near Childress, Texas, June, 1938.

Six tenant farmers without farms,
Hardman County, Texas, 1938.

She awaits the International Street Car at a corner in El Paso, Texas, to return across the bridge to Mexico. June, 1938.

Flood refugee family
near Memphis,
Tennessee, May,
1937. These people,
with all their earthly
belongings, are
bound for the lower
Rio Grande Valley,
where they hope to
pick cotton. They
came from Arkansas.

Mother and two children, on the road at
Tule Lake, California, September, 1939.

*"This is a hard way to
serve the Lord."
Oklahoma drought refugee,
California, March, 1937.*

89

*Squatters' camp on the flat where families live
during the orange-picking season, near
Porterville, California, February, 1938.*

Migrant mother,
Nipomo, California, 1936.

WILLIAM MACKEY, JR.

William Mackey, Jr., was three when he left Jacksonville, Florida, to live with his grandmother on her farm in Camden County, Georgia. The place is only fifty miles north of the Florida city where he was born in 1920. But in way of life the separation is infinitely greater.

Mackey grew up in the southernmost part of the seventy-five-mile chain of islands and marshland that makes Georgia's coast. The first explorers from Europe called the chain the Golden Isles of Guale. The influence of the white settlers from Spain, France, and England is mixed with the cultures of the indigenous Indians and the African blacks imported to be slaves. After the Civil War and Reconstruction, the area plantations that grew rice, sugarcane, cotton, and indigo disappeared as rich Northerners bought island after island. They converted the savannahs and the oak and cedar forests into pleasure resorts and hunting grounds where they could find refuge from northern winters.

Isolated as private preserves, the islands experienced few of the rapid changes that industry and technology introduced almost everywhere else in the United States. Today, however, rising taxes have forced estate owners to sell, and much of the life of fifty years ago that young William Mackey knew is vanishing.

He grew up in Scarlett, an almost all-black community. "You could get on a horse and ride for hours in any direction

and never set foot on land owned by whites," he recalls.
William had eight brothers and eight sisters. Half of them died
in early childhood. The others managed to get through grade
school, but it was a struggle to go farther. William went to
a two-room schoolhouse where one woman taught all eight
grades. She was the same teacher his mother had had, and he
was drilled in the three Rs the same way. Their textbooks
were mostly third-hand, passing through two white schools
before ending up tattered on the black children's desks.

Mackey remembers his grandmother, born in slavery, telling
him of being sold at the age of five to be the companion of
a planter's child of the same age. Too young to understand
the meaning of slavery, she thought her mother had abandoned
her. She ran away from her new owner and returned to the
plantation where her mother was held in bondage some five
miles downriver. An arrangement was worked out that permitted
the child to spend nights with her family so long as her mother
was willing to get up early enough each morning to take
her to her new master and return in time to do a full day's work
in the rice fields. Every morning for six years, she walked
with her mother five miles to the planter's house, then five miles
back in the evening, until the Civil War came and changed
everything. After Emancipation her father, Adam Sibley, served
as chief deputy sheriff of Camden County until his death ten
years later. In 1867 her husband, Charles, bought the ten-acre
farm and built with his own hands the house William Mackey
was to grow up in. Charles's father, Joe Weston, had been
a field foreman during slavery and was a fiddler renowned
throughout the region. The farm, still in the family, is now
occupied by Aaron Weston, Mackey's uncle.

"Backwoods farmers" is how city dwellers often refer to
the people who were Mackey's neighbors in Scarlett. But
it's too easy to dismiss them that way, he says. Take his
photographs of Robert Baker and his family. Baker started
work as a manual laborer at the age of eleven, cutting railroad
ties, logging, driving mules. He married a seventeen-year-old

girl in the first and worst Hoover years of the Great Depression. To make a living in those hard times, you had to go anywhere and everywhere in search of work. Baker did plastering here and painting there, fishing, lumbering, ship building and bridge building, and once worked in an ammunition dump. He had to be away from home for long periods, but he and his family remained intact and growing.

At sixty-two Robert Baker retired. With his wife he had raised fourteen children, seven boys and seven girls; two others died. Nine of the children went to college. Several, plus some sons-in-law, became teachers, and one the principal of a high school.

If he could live life over again, would Robert Baker change anything? "No," he told Mackey, "I'd go the same road and marry the same girl." That feeling about the life he made for himself is in Mackey's photographs.

From the people of Scarlett, Mackey says he learned that you should look life directly in the eye and try to deal with it on its own terms without sacrificing your dignity. "The same belief is behind my photographs. I make no attempt to be arty. I prefer the direct head-on shot, hoping the pictures will speak for themselves."

Mackey's first camera, a Brownie box, came into his hands as a birthday present when he was fifteen. By the time he left Scarlett to return to Jacksonville for high school, the camera was too battered to be of more use. He had to suspend taking pictures because he had no money for a new camera. Not until he entered military service in World War II could he afford another one.

After the war Mackey took a degree at New York University's School of Engineering and made his living as a structural engineer. All the while he used his camera in his spare time. He began making some money with it around 1955, and in 1962 he gave up engineering to live entirely by his camera. His assignments include magazine illustration, high fashion, portraiture, and photojournalism.

But what he has enjoyed doing most are documentary essays. "They demand a lot more work—both in research and shooting," he notes, "but the results, at least to me, are well worth the effort." Several summers ago he made the first of repeated journeys back to the Georgia Sea Islands and coastal mainland to begin the large-scale photo document of which the pictures in this book are a small part. He wanted to see how much that black rural scene had changed since his childhood there, and how these changes had affected the quality of life. He says, "I believe an important part of Afro-American history lies undiscovered in the folkways of southeast Georgia. Because I grew up there and much of my family is still living on the islands, I'm in an ideal position to use the camera to disclose these roots. In recent years the media have concentrated on black urban life as the central theme. The rural side has been neglected. What I've done in these summers in Georgia is not the complete story—but it is at least a beginning. It will help familiarize my own son, Patrice, with a part of his past. I'm afraid that what I've photographed will disappear in his generation."

Derry Toney, still farming in his nineties.

Condry Higginbotham, owner of the sixteen-hundred-acre
Woodbine plantation, and Dolphus Huey, the foreman.
Rice was the crop in slavery days. Now it is
truck farming produce and cattle.

Harry Way, pulpwood operator, cutting gum trees.

Gravestone at the old slave cemetery on Woodbine plantation.

99

The grandchildren of Aaron Weston.

Mrs. Letha Weston with her great-grandchild.

Gourds placed thirty feet above the chicken yard so that martins will nest in them and drive away the chicken hawks.

Tony Weston reading to his cousins.

Aaron Weston putting finishing touches on the new
West Light Baptist Church in Scarlett.
The first church was founded by ex-slaves in 1872.

*Robert Baker, before the Mission
House on the coast near St.
Marys, Georgia. The mission was
built by slaves in 1572.*

MARTIN SCHNEIDER

What could be more of a civil right than the right to breathe clean air? How inalienable is the right to life, liberty, and the pursuit of happiness when we are suckled on genocidal air?''

One man—the photographer Martin Schneider—has been asking these questions for nearly ten years.

''Doesn't the Declaration of Independence hold true for America today?'' he wants to know. And then he cites the passages that strike home:

He [King George] has plundered our seas, ravaged our Coasts, burnt our towns, and destroyed the lives of our people . . . . mankind are more disposed to suffer, while evils are sufferable, than to right themselves by abolishing the forms to which they are accustomed. But when a long train of abuses and usurpations, pursuing invariably the same Object, evinces a design to reduce them under absolute Despotism, it is their right, it is their duty, to throw off such Government, and to provide new Guards for their future security.

''How less a despotism is tyranny from Detroit than tyranny from London?'' Schneider asks. ''How much more representative is government that smiles today upon those who are more subtly, but not less surely, plundering our seas, ravaging our coasts, burning our towns, and destroying the lives of our people? It is physically possible to live without free speech,

free press, peaceable assembly, redress of grievances,
citizenship rights. It is physically *impossible* to live with
poisoned air."

Schneider's concern about air pollution goes back to 1964
when the Surgeon General of the U. S. Public Health Service
saw his photo essay on tuberculosis and asked if he would
document air pollution as a basis for legislation against it.
Schneider said he knew nothing about pollution and would
want time to study it. He saw the assignment as an unlimited
opportunity to use and expand skills he had already developed.
More—it was a chance to explore new areas in his own search
for identity. Out of this effort would come a sustaining sense
of fulfillment.

Always a thorough investigator, he set about mastering
the subject of air pollution. Then he faced an even harder task:
how to make people see what they cannot see. War, hunger,
child labor, racial discrimination—the signs of these evils
are visible, and the camera can catch and record them. But
pollution? And what it does to the environment and to its
human victims? How can the camera document this?

Schneider gave his enormous energy and ingenuity to the
problem, and taught himself how. In the opinion of many, his
achievement is in the great tradition of the photographers
who are his models—Riis, Hine, Lange, Eugene Smith. "If we
are still breathing ten years from now," said the *New York
Times* of Schneider, "some of our thanks will be due to him."

Such thanks are not earned easily when you are a photographer crusading against powerful economic and political
interests. Schneider has been put down as a lunatic, Boy
Scout, fanatic, troublemaker. Bad words—and worse—do not
stop him. He relishes repeating the stories of his opposition,
and uses attacks against him to dramatize his continuing
crusade against pollution.

Schneider was born in New York City in 1927. His father was a sculptor who worked in wood and taught his son how to use woodworking tools, a skill he adapted years later to the mastery of machine tool operation. Severe asthmatic bronchitis made young Schneider an invalid. For a few years he was unable to go to school and had to be given lessons by a teacher in his home. To build up his strength, he worked summers on dairy and poultry farms. At eighteen, near the end of World War II, he was drafted. Concealing the record of his medical disability, he astonishingly became a paratrooper.

After military service he entered Brooklyn College, planning to become a psychologist. He was interested in the functional expression of art in all its forms. When he wanted to try photograms, he took a photography course at the college under Walter Rosenblum, who introduced him to the documentary work of Hine and Riis. Until then he hadn't realized that the camera could be used to make social statements. Rosenblum remembers him as "a quiet young man, working in the school's photo lab with meticulous craftsmanship."

Schneider had committed himself to photography when a routine medical exam revealed he had tuberculosis and must undergo medical treatment. He asked the staff of Montefiore Hospital to let him use his camera to document everything about his disease, from the time a person discovers the bacillus is active in his body through the course of treatment and rehabilitation. From 1953 to 1957 he shot many thousands of photographs and wrote hundreds of pages, documenting long-term illness as a way of life. "Instead of giving in to the illness," says Rosenblum, "he used it as the subject matter for a brilliant photo essay on his own experiences."

What helped to shape him around the same time in the 1950s were the biweekly gatherings of a small group of photographers meeting at Lou Bernstein's and their own homes. They not only looked at one another's work but probed deep into themselves to discover their motivations and their values. "Why were we shooting what we were? What did it mean? They were rough sessions," Schneider says. "No one imitated anyone else. We wanted to get deeper into ourselves."

It was the respiratory specialists he came to know during his illness who ultimately led Schneider to his intensive work on air pollution. His first assignment was in the New York-New Jersey metropolitan area. He made still photographs and a film on the thin budget of two thousand dollars, borrowing almost ten times that amount to carry out the project properly. After that came a film for Senator Edmund Muskie's subcommittee on Air and Water Pollution. This work led to a contract with *Life* magazine to do a photo document on pollution as a national problem. It promised to let him recover some of the losses he had sustained.

What happened while he traveled the country to dig out the facts startled Schneider and was the beginning of the legend that has grown up about him. While working in Florida, for instance, he was deterred at gunpoint from documenting pollution. His specially adapted Land Rover, which he had equipped with a complete pollution detection lab, was sabotaged. "And my pictures were robbed from an Air Express office to prevent *Life* from publishing them. Then, after I retook them, they disappeared mysteriously from the hands of *Life*'s managing editor!" He also tells of "an armed employee of a . . . phosphate plant, posing as a sheriff, trying to intimidate me while I was working to expose the plant's pollutants."

The phosphate industry located near Tampa, says Schneider, "emits a combination of sulfuric and hydrofluoric acids that kills cattle and destroys the citrus crops on nearby ranches and farms. They also produce ulceration of the respiratory tract and vomiting in humans." Schneider obtained photos of clouds of sulfuric acid about fifty feet deep and extending over five square miles.

Later Schneider, together with consumer spokesman Ralph Nader, appeared on NBC's Today show. Schneider charged the phosphate industry with killing some thirty-five thousand cattle, destroying some twenty-five million dollars' worth of citrus crops, and causing serious illness in people—facts taken from the testimony of both the United States and the Florida Department of Agriculture. The industry has never been able to refute his charges and has never pressed any libel suit against him.

A year after Schneider had completed his assignment, *Life* ran a twelve-page color spread of his pictures revealing the polluted atmosphere—but none of his photos of pollution's devastating effect upon people and animals. Instead of using his text, the magazine ran its own, watering down his carefully documented research. "A monumental whitewash," he calls it. Schneider is not the kind of photographer ready to settle for half the truth or a handsome fee.

One of his ideas for demonstrating the phosphate pollution problem shows how fertile his imagination is and how inventive his mind in carrying out his design. The most sensational picture he conceived in Florida was intended for *Life*'s cover. (It was the picture that disappeared twice.) Schneider had taken the carcasses of cows, autopsied to prove cause of death, and mounted them on public land in front of a phosphate plant. When he turned his fluoroscope and shortwave ultraviolet equipment on them, they revealed the deadly concentrations of fluorides deposited in bone tissue, in grisly, luminous confirmation of such pollution-caused death. At midnight Schneider projected the image of one of the vivid skulls above the plant, against a bank of smog. Then he photographed that image. The result: a powerful photograph showing the plant's fumes pouring up from the stacks, and above them the ghastly skull of one of the victims killed by those fumes.

In the course of his work Schneider has developed no love for politicians. He finds them—with few exceptions—so compromised by the conflict of interest between the public welfare and their own political ambitions that their work is ineffective or worse. When he is accused of bias against industry, Schneider denies it. "My work is to reveal the technology of industry which offers alternatives, and which they are suppressing," he says. Car manufacturers know how to save lives by introducing the gas turbine or steam engines, he points out, but they don't do it. And the electric power utilities have the means to clear up the pollution they are responsible for, if they wanted to. "Air pollution throughout the nation could be ended permanently in less than three months, without it costing the taxpayers one cent," he has said.

Schneider does not consider himself primarily a photographer. Photography is simply work he does in the course of functioning as an environmental consultant. "I use the camera as Lewis Hine did as a sociologist to document the conditions he felt were so intolerable—the children working in coal mines. . . ." His aim is to involve concerned people throughout the country to find solutions, "the solutions the industries have, that they just don't care about." He believes that if industries acted, they would make more money, not less.

What would make them act? "Citizen lobbies," says Schneider, "functioning in every city hall, every state capitol, and in Washington—every day of the year, not just one-time marches." He sees his photographs as a means of rousing popular concern, to show people there is something they can *do*. He also believes in the power of mass withholding of consumer debts payable to utilities (the money to be held in escrow) and in boycotts and other means of economic pressure to force industries and their political mouthpieces to act in the public interest.

He is hardly out to cripple industry. "My concern," he explains, "is keeping *everyone* alive—the employees in the factories, the management, the people who live in those communities. The livelihood of all of them is dependent upon the companies." Tough antipollution laws and tough enforcement policies will benefit everyone, he believes. He cites as an example the Bethlehem Steel mill in Los Angeles that was shut down by government order while electric furnaces were installed in place of the open hearth. Now its employees are healthier and so are its profits. The pressures applied against a complacent management by forces that include a concerned photographer like Schneider can go far in solving ecological problems. *Breath of Death* is the title of Schneider's forthcoming book on the subject.

Schneider shrugs off complimentary remarks about his one-man crusade. It's not *his* crusade, he says. "I'm only helping to publicize the otherwise suppressed achievements of scientific research that provide desperately sought answers in ecology. Any time you get involved in doing something seriously, and you stay with it, they call you a nut."

What Schneider has received for what he has done is very little. His small income is derived chiefly from teaching college courses in ecology and in photography and film making on the theme of "The Angry Lens." He has turned down commercial offers by magazines and television because he considered what they wanted him to do "ecological pornography, with no socially redeeming value." Editorial programs he has done for TV "have been either severely censored or taken off the air."

One editor, trying to induce him to agree to a censored layout of his work that had already been sent to the printer, pleaded that "half a lie is better than a whole lie." When Schneider pulled his entire piece out, the man said, "You must be independently wealthy."

"No," Schneider replied, "I'm independently poor."

New York City on a relatively clear day. The rotor of a U.S. Coast Guard helicopter identifies Con Edison's Ravenswood facility in Queens.

New York City during an air pollution emergency in 1966. The plume of smoke from Con Edison's Ravenswood facility appears to be in violation of the law. The mandatory fuel for the plant is natural gas, which burns without producing smoke. The local death rate during this emergency rose one hundred percent, with five hundred dying.

Central Park on Thanksgiving Day, 1966. This is not at sunset. The view is due south at 2:30 p.m. The skaters in the Wollman Rink were oblivious to the five hundred fellow New Yorkers who died that day, double the number of deaths in the city on an average day.

Traffic on Pennsylvania Avenue during the morning rush hours in Washington, D.C.

The identical scene at the same time of the same day. By use of gas analyzer optics, the traffic is rendered invisible, while the invisible nitrogen oxides (a thousand times deadlier than carbon monoxide) are clearly revealed flooding the street.

*Not even the heart of the Rockies is immune from deadly pollution.
The daily inversion over the pulp mill at Missoula, Montana, produces
a haunting mushroom cloud containing mercaptans that smell like
rotting cabbage.*

*The family clothesline full of brand-new apparel set up
on the roof of a steelworker's home in the Chicago area.*

The same clothesline after three months' exposure to emissions from Chicago's steel mills. Disintegration is measurable not in inches, but in feet of material. Other test lines hung with identical new garments in different parts of the city revealed only fading— no destruction.

About seventy percent of the United States market for phosphates is supplied by the industry in Florida's Polk and Hillsborough counties. Projected above one of the plants emitting its clouds of pollutants is the image of a skull taken from one of the cows autopsied to prove that they had died from the industrial pollutants. The photographic technique employed reveals the deadly fluorides deposited in the bone tissue of the skull. Schneider's original photo, shot in Florida for a Life cover, disappeared twice.

*Martin Schneider's father
dying of emphysema.*

FUNG LAM

What was best about high school, says Fung Lam, was the
time he spent *away* from Brooklyn Tech. His freshman year was
the only one he devoted exclusively to schoolwork. "I did all
the things a good little freshman had to do," he says, and got
a high average to prove it. It only made him feel depressed.
His whole life revolved around school—or more precisely,
grades. If the school records burned, he wondered, would he
pass into oblivion? Were grades all there was to Fung Lam?
"There's more to me than a permanent record card," he
told himself. But what?

He plunged into sports, publications, clubs. They kept him
busy, but unsatisfied. They were harmless activities, but
what did they add up to?

He began going to a discussion group that met at the
neighborhood library. It focused on the communications media
and the way they reflected what was going on in the world
—an escalating war, political assassinations, racial unrest,
pollution. The discussions awakened him to the creative
potential of photography as a news medium and an art form.

Lam was no stranger to the camera. He had taken it up as
a hobby in the seventh grade. The basic process seemed
magical: the creation of images. But it took money to process
his pictures, and Lam came from a family that had little to

spare. He was born in Hong Kong in 1954 and was brought from China to the United States at the age of four. He grew up in Chinatown on the Lower East Side of New York. An immigrant, he knew no English at first, but discovered how much he could learn by absorbing the countless images around him —in newspapers, magazines, and books, on television and in the movies, on the billboards and the posters in subways and buses. All were visual clues to a strange environment.

Unable to afford film processing, Lam set about doing it himself and learned that he could get better results than the corner drugstore through his self-taught darkroom techniques. Now he saw there was no magic in it—you simply had to master your craft. In the summer after his freshman year he worked in a camera plant. He learned enough about photomechanics during lunch and coffee breaks to be able to build an experimental camera from junked parts.

That fall he began taking pictures of people he saw along New York streets, looking for simple everyday scenes of life. A librarian friend saw his work and liked it enough to arrange a traveling exhibition in the city's library system. Only fourteen years old then, Lam had audaciously priced his pictures at twenty-five dollars a print, figuring nobody would buy them anyhow. The first day of the show from a corner of the room he watched how strangers walked up to his photographs and smiled or laughed, taking pleasure in what he had done. He was just as astonished when numbers of them bought prints—enough to enable him to more than break even and purchase some equipment.

It was now that Lam was lucky enough to meet the man who would have the greatest influence upon him, Benedict J. Fernandez. Raised in New York's Puerto Rican Harlem, Fernandez had become a photographer distinguished for his award-winning documents of protest and dissent. Lam joined Fernandez's Photo Film Workshop. There young people from thirteen to twenty, mostly drawn from the city's ghettos, are given a free education in photography.

Fernandez's goal is not to make young people photographers. "All I'm trying to do," he has said, "is to make people interested in life. I think photography is a good excuse to go somewhere, to be nosy, to be curious, to get yourself involved, to expand your thoughts." Fernandez has found that many young people have talent, but don't know where to go with it.

His workshop was what Fung Lam needed. It plunged the boy deep into picture making. He spent delighted hours with others like himself, trying to master the camera. For four years he worked at it, both learning and teaching. That was how Fernandez believed such young people grew the best. By being both teachers and students of one another, they had to deal with themselves, to take responsibility, to find out how to perform so they would earn the respect of the others. Eventually Fung Lam became an apprentice to Fernandez.

Photography swung him head-on into a life he would never have met normally. The camera made his days hectic. There was still Brooklyn Tech, the Photo Film Workshop, and an after-class job at the New School as lab technician and teaching assistant in the photography department—and homework on top of all that. Weekends he went off to this city or that to cover a peace march or a civil-rights demonstration. The more he did, the more he seemed able to do. The next summer he won a scholarship to study at the Center of the Eye in Aspen, Colorado. Publications and organizations began giving him photo assignments and printing his work.

The load was enormous. The world outside high school was taking a lot out of him—and putting something more in. Most of the time he wouldn't be home until midnight, arriving dead tired. But in spite of the strain, he said, "I felt alive and happy. For the first time I was doing something concrete, useful, and creative." *Scope,* one of Scholastic's many publications, gave a full issue to his photo essay on Chinatown.

His protest pictures were exhibited at Westbeth Gallery in New York City to raise funds for the antiwar movement. His study of Harlem children appeared in a textbook series on ghetto life. And the Children's Aid Society used his pictures in ads, posters, and pamphlets to raise money.

The summer of 1971 began with work at the New School. Then he went to Nashville, Tennessee, to photograph country-and-western stars such as Johnny Cash and Roy Acuff. Back in New York City, he helped the Guggenheim Museum with an inner city children's project. And then came an arrangement with the Children's Aid Society to work for three weeks at the Wagon Road Camp for handicapped children in Chappaqua, New York. A small grant from the International Fund for Concerned Photography gave him the means to do a thorough job. He wanted to see what becomes of people who are not "created equal" physically. How does a handicapped child grow? How does he relate to other children and to the adults who work with him?

Through his camera Lam captured the way the camp provided the children and their counselors "with some beautiful moments along with hard ones. The experience taught them to commit themselves to life, rather than escape from it. Many learned that the best moments, no matter how few, are worth withstanding the hardships for." Lam says he saw that summer how life at best is an equilibrium of good times and bad.

From his photography at camp came an exhibition that has traveled to several major cities and universities across the country, and that won for Lam the Photography for Youth Foundation Award.

Lam entered Harvard College as a freshman in the fall of 1972. He does not intend to earn his living as a photographer. For him it is not a life's work, but a creative release. He is taking a premedical course and hopes to be a doctor *and* a photographer. Photography could be his livelihood, he knows, but the material on which he could make the most money would

not necessarily satisfy his inner needs. What he might want
to do might not be what people would pay for. With his plan,
he will have both—"medicine as a profession where you're
actually helping your fellow human beings, and photography as
a form of personal expression."

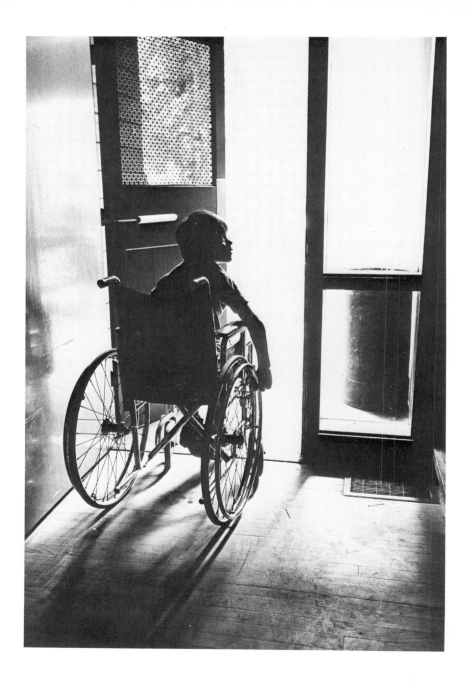

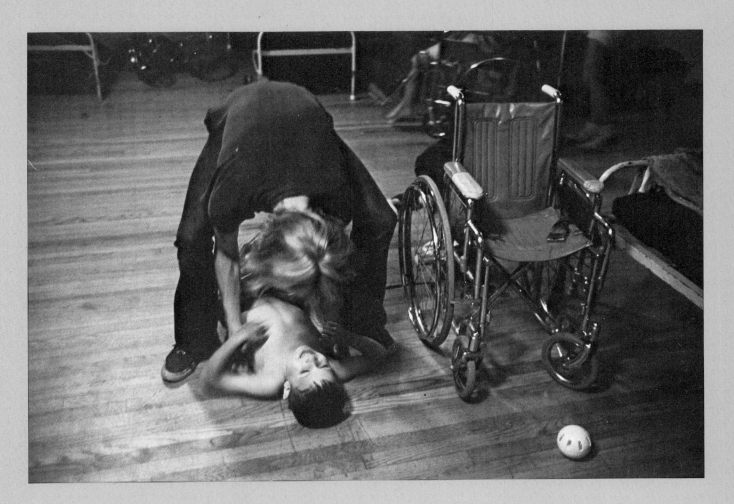

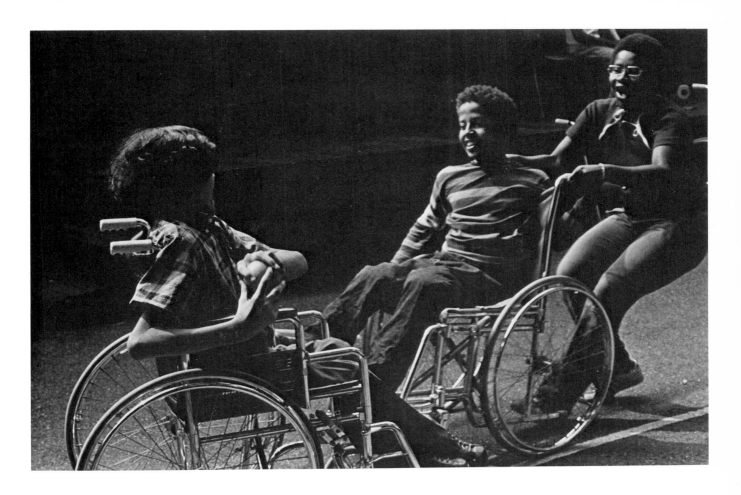

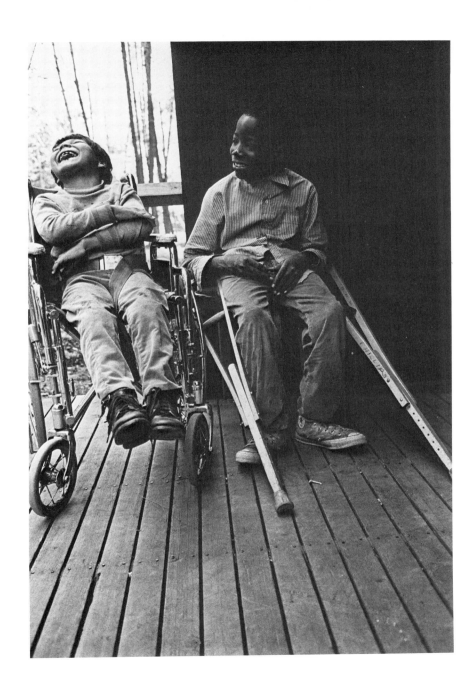

MICHAEL ABRAMSON

Month after month Michael Abramson followed the Young Lords with camera and tape recorder. At the end he emerged with a striking example of what committed photography can be. His book *Palante: Young Lords Party* shows, in Abramson's mind, "what it means in deep personal terms to be a revolutionary in this society."

Abramson was born in Plainfield, New Jersey, in 1944. At seventeen, he went to Kenyon College in Ohio and then on to the University of Chicago for a master's degree in the history of culture. While at college he started taking pictures as a hobby, shooting almost anything to gain experience. He went on to graduate school because he thought he wanted to teach, but by the time he earned the degree, he had changed his mind.

Not knowing what to do, he came to New York City and found a job in a fashion photography studio. The work gave him the chance to learn the necessary techniques. He decided he would use them to make himself into a photojournalist. But to shoot what? No one would give assignments to an unknown. He looked about for something with political meaning.

He happened to be on the scene the day the Young Lords took over a Methodist church in Spanish Harlem and renamed it The People's Church—it was December 28, 1969. For eleven

days they ran free clothing drives, free breakfast and free
health programs, a liberation school, and a day care center.
At night they offered the neighborhood free entertainment
—movies, music, poetry. Three thousand came to The People's
Church in that short time.

Now the newspapers had spread word of the Young Lords
everywhere throughout the country as a new kind of political
force. The Young Lords opened more branches, started a
newspaper called *Palante* and a radio program with the same
name. They extended their action to include lead poisoning and
tuberculosis detection programs, plunging into the field of
health to meet the needs of both the patients and the hospital
workers—most of whom were black and Puerto Rican. They
also threw their energies into the struggle to stop oppression of
brothers and sisters in prison. However, their central political
goal is the liberation of Puerto Rico. They believe it can be won
only by combating the racism that divides people of color
and by uniting Puerto Ricans on the island and the mainland.
Novelist Richard Wright once said what they believe: "You're
either a victim or a rebel."

Only twenty-five when he started his essay on the Young
Lords, Abramson soon began to move in a new direction
for photographers. Like his forerunners, he was socially
conscious. But his camera focused on people struggling,
not suffering. Abramson respects the images of the poor and
the deprived that Riis and Hine and others have made. But
he points out that sixty years later, countless millions here and
abroad remain "enslaved in conditions of poverty, human
degradation, and oppression. It is time for photographers to
stop photographing the victims of America and begin to record
the struggle of those who fight against their victimization."

As he worked with the Young Lords, Abramson became
committed to them as individual people and as an organization.
He never pretends to objectivity. Whatever detachment he
may once have felt gave ground to increasingly intimate

identification with the young Puerto Ricans in the birthing of their movement. He was not out to amass the images of victims and add their suffering to an already overwhelming mountain of pity. Nor was he documenting the demonstrations of nameless thousands with stacks of prints headed for the dusty archives of historians. Instead, his work is a witness to a moral commitment made to specific people fighting to change oppressive conditions. At the same time that he makes his case for the Young Lords, he documents what created their revolution and what makes the struggle so fulfilling of their humanity.

As his work with the Young Lords became known, Abramson began to get occasional assignments from the media—usually to photograph street gangs or violence in Harlem or the south Bronx—places where other photographers were not eager to go.

In the fall of 1972 he went to West Virginia to work on a documentary film about the coal miners. A second book of his has appeared, a brief photo essay on Fayette County, Tennessee, where blacks had built a tent city when they were evicted from their homes for trying to vote.

Cauldwell Avenue, Bronx, New York,
November, 1970.

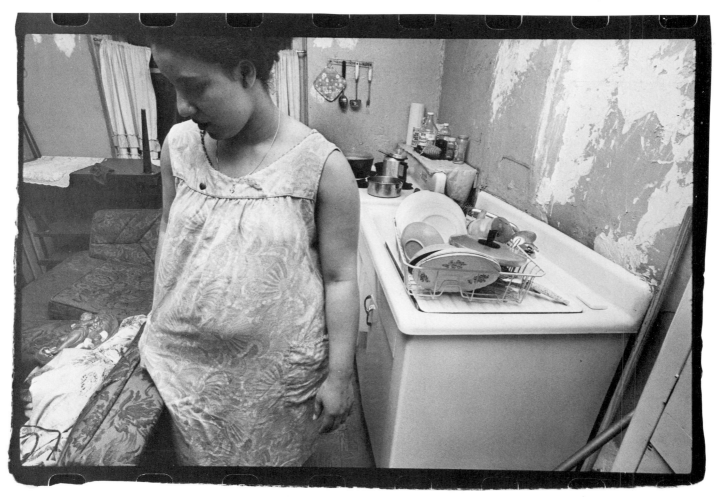

Cauldwell Avenue, Bronx, New York, November, 1970.

Puerto Rican community,
Newark, New Jersey,
September, 1970.

Cauldwell Avenue, Bronx, New York, November, 1970.

Outside The People's Church,
June, 1970.

145

Explaining the armed seizure of The People's Church,
October, 1970.

*March to commemorate Ponce massacre
of 1937, Bronx, New York,
March 21, 1971.*

*Free breakfast program, Second People's Church,
October, 1970.*

Carrying clothes to the First People's Church,
January, 1970.

Young Lords Richie Rodriguez, Denise Oliver, Bobby Lemus.
June, 1970.

IRA NOWINSKI

The Joyce Hotel had to come down, said the newspaper, because Shell Oil wanted to put a gas station on the spot. The hotel was occupied by elderly men, ninety of them, mostly pensioners who had lived there many years. Now they had a fifteen-day eviction notice. Pack up and get out. Find another place to live.

When Ira Nowinski read that story, he decided to go down to the Joyce to photograph what was happening. It was March of 1971. For six months he had been taking pictures of a family as a project for a class in photography taught by Richard Conrat at the San Francisco Art Institute. Through Conrat, who had studied under Dorothea Lange, Nowinski had learned to get close to people. "My work with the camera had improved," he said, "but I wanted to make photos that would have more meaning, not just to myself, but to other people. I wanted a social theme."

On his first visit to the Joyce he met Amanda Fisher, a young lawyer for the Neighborhood Legal Assistance Foundation. She was there to help the tenants organize to resist the eviction. Nowinski started to work with her, providing photos for her to use in court actions. And he began to learn about the way elderly people live, and how to reveal it through the camera.

There were almost four thousand single elderly pensioners living in San Francisco's Yerba Buena area in the South-of-Market district. Many of them were retired trade unionists who had been part of the progressive labor movements of the twenties and thirties. Living in the district's many hotels, they had built a system of mutual support.

Far better than the bureaucratic, impersonal Welfare Department was their own form of self-help. It ensured that no one went hungry or lay sick in his room without aid or comfort. A network of friendships held people together and kept them going. To tear down the Joyce—or any of Yerba Buena that the city's Redevelopment Agency wanted to raze—was to do away with sound buildings serving a useful purpose. It was profiting the rich at the expense of the poor, while the city and federal governments did little or nothing to plan for decent and safe replacement housing.

Most of the tenants of the Joyce had left before they could be organized to fight back. So the Joyce was torn down. But the legal battle went on to stop the Redevelopment Agency's displacement tactics, which were placing the elderly into worse housing at higher rents.

Nowinski's experience, helping the friends he made in the Joyce, gave his work new dimensions. He was not only documenting the problems that millions of America's senior citizens share today. "I was using my photos politically, forcing people in authority to take affirmative action."

It had been a long, roundabout way to a goal discovered at the age of twenty-nine. Ira Nowinski was born in New York in 1942. The oldest of four children, he grew up in Brooklyn. His father was a piping engineer. His grandmother, who owned an antique shop and painted, began taking him to art museums when he was a small boy. The family moved to New Rochelle, New York, when he was ready to start high school. There young Nowinski got most of his pleasure out of painting.

But he also became absorbed in herpetology and with a
school friend earned money by importing and selling snakes.
It made him think he ought to be a field zoologist, so he
gave up art for zoology when he went to Michigan State
University.

His grades at college were poor, however, and on his return
to New York he worked for a stock broker. Two years later
he visited college friends in Detroit who were social workers.
Because he didn't like selling on Wall Street, he took a
qualifying exam for social work. When he passed, he found
a job in Detroit.

That, too, lasted briefly. Within a year he was wandering
through Mexico and Central America, living on his savings and
what he made by catching snakes and lizards and shipping
them to animal dealers in Florida and New York. All that came
out of this period was the knowledge that he liked to travel.
He still had not settled on a career. Again he took a job on Wall
Street to support himself.

But in the summer of 1968 he borrowed an old Kodak
Retina and walked the streets and parks, shooting almost
anything he saw. When he had developed the first few rolls of
film, he said, "I knew this was what I could get involved
in. So I saved my money, bought a Pentax, then quit my job.
To become a photographer, I knew I had to concentrate on the
camera. I realized I needed freedom, even at the price of
instability, if I was not to be the weekend photographer I saw
so much of in New York."

He made an agreement with people importing birds and
animals, and set out for Thailand. There he bought from dealers
and shipped the birds and animals back to New York. He
continued taking pictures all the time, discovering depth and
the use of light, but he did not seek to publish anything.

Returning to New York, he became a floor assistant and
delivery man for a fashion photographer. He didn't like it, but

he learned a respect for technical proficiency. Four months later he left for San Francisco, where he began classes in photography at the Art Institute. In a year he was competent enough to be accepted into graduate school as a candidate for the Master of Fine Arts degree.

Nowinski enjoyed studying at the Institute. "It has a free atmosphere, and you can try what you like without worrying about grades. I like it, too, because it's a fine arts school where you can get to know painters, sculptors, and printmakers as well as photographers."

At the Institute Richard Conrat wanted his students to work with a set of disciplines, Nowinski said. "First we would photograph the same family, week after week, bringing in only contacts or work prints. We were more than observers; we came to know the people, which gave our pictures richer meaning. By staying with the one family, we had the chance to realize what opportunities we had missed and to go back to get those photos later. I learned how to handle my camera, using one film and developer under basically the same circumstances. I got used to reading the contact sheets, which would become invaluable in work I did later. We also gave the photos to the family, discussing them, getting feedback as we went along. The end result was a book of photos put together for the family, an exercise that showed me how photos can be made to work together rather than as single images."

When Nowinski went on to photograph the people in the Joyce Hotel and in other places in Yerba Buena, he began to discover many things he didn't know about the aged. First, their many problems with health and how it affects everything else. "They have a different outlook on sociability," he said. "They don't like crowds, but prefer to be alone or with a few friends. They are so used to being ignored by society, by family, by young people, to being cheated or robbed, that they are very suspicious. It takes a lot of patience before the barriers come down. Young people have to make the initial moves. Once they trust you, they are very open, showing their feelings if you share yours with them. When you become friends, you're often astonished by the life stories you hear."

Through his work with old people Nowinski received a grant from the National Endowment for the Arts to photograph the Yerba Buena project. Now he has met many lawyers and community organizers involved in social struggle. From time to time his pictures are used on television specials as well as in court proceedings to document what is happening.

Nowinski makes his living as staff photographer for the biweekly newspaper *The San Francisco Progress,* which covers community news. "It is a committed paper," he explains, "and we often wind up fighting city hall. I don't make much money at it, but our stories and photos balance the one-sided coverage the big papers give hot issues. I feel this work, too, has social use."

Nowinski uses a 35mm Leica and Tri-X, relies only on natural light, and prints full frame. "I spend a lot of time developing my ideas, determining how to link one with another, to give a theme the most powerful expression I can," he says. He also takes a great deal of trouble to arrange photos in the order that will tell a story best, and at the same time evoke a flow of feeling. If some of the images don't seem just right—the composition or the light not what they should be—he will go back for a better photo.

He explains this meticulousness: "I feel I'm not just documenting a subject. I'm giving it a personal interpretation and a political thrust. That combination is the most important esthetic I can think of."

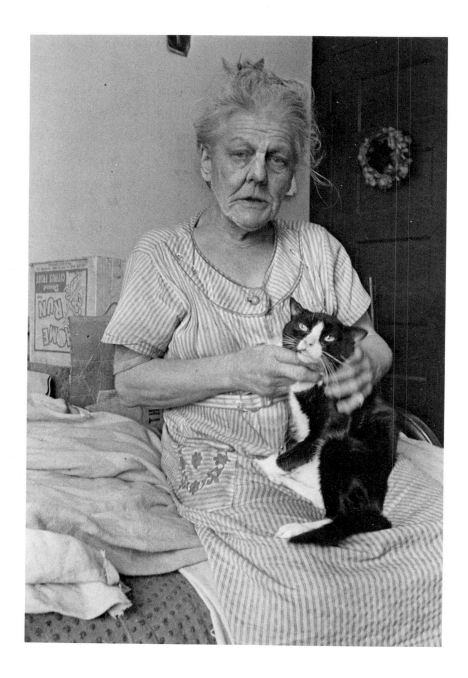

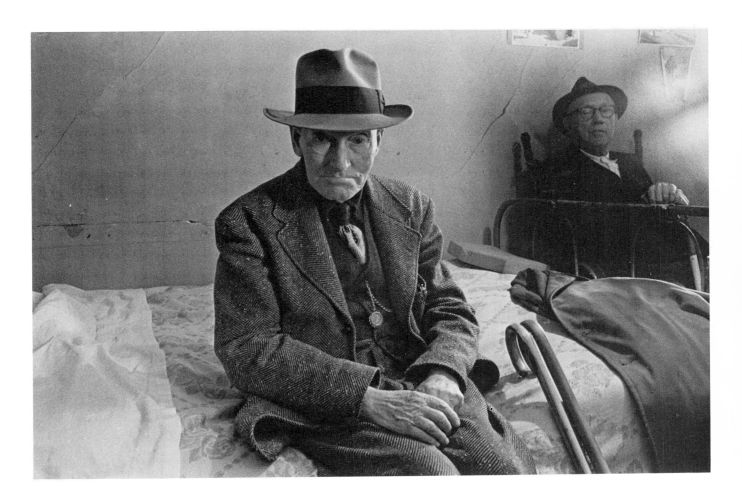

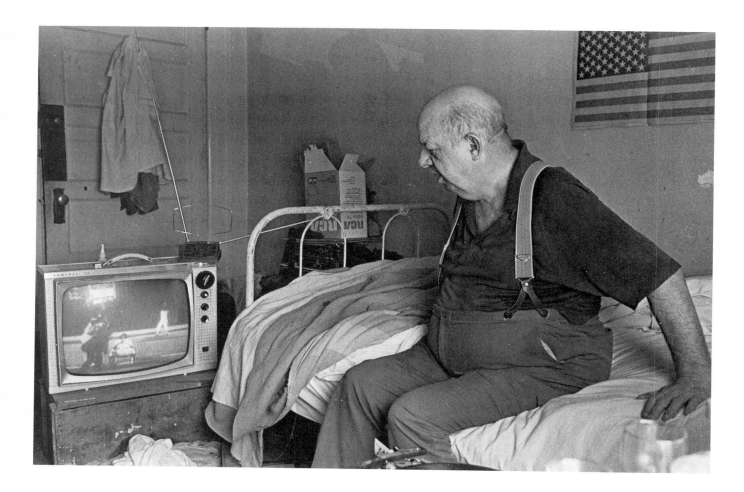

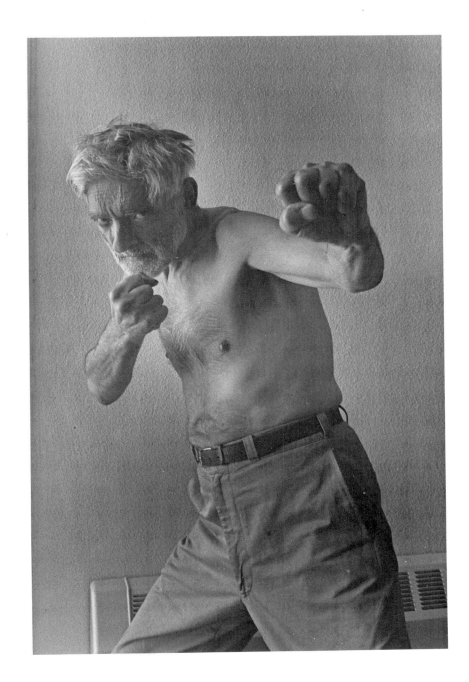

MORRIE CAMHI

For a dozen years Morrie Camhi had been running his own studio, devoted to advertising photography. Blue-chip accounts generated high income. It was a comfortable way to live —working with models and art directors and big campaigns. To many in the world of photography, this was the top of the totem pole. If that needed confirmation, there was the invitation to exhibit his work at the Los Angeles Museum in a Photography West show. Camhi won an award. But all this no longer was enough to make him happy.

When the news came that Robert Kennedy had been assassinated, the shock crystallized the vague disquiet that had seized the photographer. Now he began to probe his feelings about himself and his work. What were his photographs about? What did they mean? He asked himself which of those he was making right now would stand the test of time. What ones would be worth looking at a hundred years from now, ten years from now?

"I didn't go through my negative file to find out," he said. "I didn't have to. It was obvious that maybe one in two thousand would pass such a test. Our society was in turmoil. The Kennedy killing was only one of countless terrible events going on around me. But my camera, instead of interpreting movements and people that were dynamic forces in our life, was photographing bottles of Scotch, dream trailers, and the newest computers.''

He sold his studio and started on a new life, a new way of using his camera.

He was forty years old when he made that decision.

Camhi, born in New York City in 1928, got into photography by an ironic route. His high school friends were excited about photography and formed a neighborhood club. He didn't join. He scarcely knew which end of a camera was the front. The father of one of his friends, a printer, promised to run off some stationery for the camera club. Camhi's pals, hearing he was moving to Los Angeles, begged him to start another club when he got to California so they could print ''From Coast to Coast'' under their club's name.

At Manual Arts High School in Los Angeles, there was no photo club. Camhi formed one to keep his promise. He still knew nothing about photography. But his club members didn't realize it. They popped endless questions at him—which camera did he like best? What subjects were his favorites? He blurted out lies to cover his ignorance. Then the club decided to hold an exhibit at the end of the semester. Camhi still owned no camera and had not yet taken a single photograph.

Now he had to produce. He found a job in a photo supply house. ''A wonderful guy named Coleman Schwartz was a technical representative for the company,'' Camhi recalls. ''He sold me an old postcard-size Speed Graphic with a good lens.'' Camhi spent hours in the library reading up on photography and hours more talking photography with Schwartz. He bought chemicals, film, paper, and went out to shoot. ''I just had to do well, or I couldn't face my friends.''

His first pictures were, he says, ''reasonably acceptable.'' He had redeemed the lies. Still he had no intention of becoming a photographer. He dreamed of being a lawyer. The Army drafted him and assigned him to the Signal Corps as a photographer. He served two years. He notes, "I did something awfully unusual for the Army; I decided to take everything seriously." He shot his assignments the very best way he knew how. "It was a kind of private school of photography, a school I ran for myself at Camp Roberts. The Army's standards, unfortunately, were not too high, but I tried to raise the standards and enlarge my own knowledge of photography."

Discharged from the Army, he entered the University of California at Los Angeles as a theater arts major. He began to think of directing as a career. But at college he met his wife-to-be, Lynn, and soon after they married she was pregnant. He was working his way through school on two part-time jobs, as waiter and photo lab technician. Now he desperately needed full-time work to support his growing family. The photo studio offered him the manager's job, and he took it. For six years he stayed on while it grew into a profitable commercial enterprise.

Wanting independence, Camhi left and opened his own studio. It was then that he got into the glamorous world of advertising photography. After a dozen years of success, he woke up to the realization that this was not enough for him. With his wife's full support he dropped out of business and began teaching photography at the City College of San Francisco. His hope was that it would provide a basic income, give him a chance to impart what he had learned, and leave him enough time to carry out his own photographic projects.

Teaching proved to be a good thing to do. The only drawback was that the free time was never enough. Still, he has been able to tackle assignments he likes and shoot his own photo essays "independent of whether or not there is money at the end of the line." He works with his camera when he thinks the theme is worth exploring and the images will be significant. "That's how I like to have it," he says.

His photo essay "The Farm Workers" is a case in point.

The press had long been reporting the workers' struggle
to organize. In his travels around California Camhi had often
encountered the Chicano migratory workers. What he had
sensed about their lives hadn't come through in the photographs
he had seen. He began to wonder why. Many photographers
had portrayed the great personalities linked to the struggle
—Cesar Chavez, Robert Kennedy—or the dramatic events—
the strike actions and demonstrations—which had news value.
In the face of the thousands of photographs already made,
what more could be added? What was there still to say that
would be different and meaningful?

Camhi "remembered the photos of the ramshackle huts, the
miserable sanitation, the tattered clothing, the soulful eyes
that seemed the very symbol of poverty." And then he knew
what was the matter. "By responding symbolically, I saw
we had tended to respond to a visual cliché that robbed a
valiant people of their individuality and complexity. We had
sensed the sledgehammer logic of their condition, muttered
something unassailable about how bad it was, somehow
felt relieved to have paid our sociological dues."

Not pathos, not news events, not the big personalities, would
be his subject, but people, these particular people with their
tenacity, their strength, their dedication, their ability to think
through their problems, to measure the risks and the rewards
of their actions. Their day-to-day activities were not so different
from those of many others, Camhi felt. What was special
was "the dignity and commitment that's unique to aspiring
people, the kind of belief and hope others of us have left
behind."

His problem was to make his photographs reflect honestly
the natural quality of the Chicanos. But by the time he began,
they had been the targets of a thousand cameras. "It was
hard not to photograph photographers, there were so many
milling around the union hall," recalls Camhi. And the people
in and around the movement were so used to the camera

that they would frequently strike a pose or "present" them-selves. Camhi made himself part of the movement. He spent a dozen and more hours a day in the union hall, on the picket line, making picket signs, driving pickets here and there, carrying messages. And when he saw a reaction he felt was true to the life of the movement, he took his picture.

Worn out at night, he'd flop on a cot, unable to sleep, trying to make sense out of what was going on. "What have I really seen?" he asked himself. "What was I really photographing? How was it different from what I had thought I was going to photograph before I got here?" What it all boiled down to, he said, was keeping an open mind.

Most of the time, while he was with the Chicanos, he was only another part of a group, doing some work. He feels that's important in this kind of photography. "It's not necessary to *be* a farm worker, but it *is* necessary to know what being one is all about, to feel some of the same emotions, some of the same heights, some of the same depths."

Having an open mind doesn't mean you lack a point of view, he said. "There isn't such a thing as a completely objective or 'honest' photograph. Turn several photographers loose on a situation: one will make it look brutal, another romantic, a third like cold data. Which of the photographers is really honest? Maybe all, maybe none. I think the only valid test is that the photographer be true to what he sees. What he sees will be conditioned by what he is, who he has been."

What Camhi is wary of is photographic hypocrisy. He explains, "It would have been easy, in the farm worker essay, to get a series of heartrending, tear-jerking photos. Awfully easy and I was tempted. I knew they'd be saleable, they'd be attention-grabbers, and I resisted the impulse because that wasn't what it was all about."

Camhi does not like to have his photographs captioned. He'd rather have the image speak for itself. He doesn't mind if the images are ambiguous. The image a photographer captures cannot be as precise as mathematics, he says. "Trying to make it that precise takes away some of the subtle flavor we come back to strong photographs to sense again. Poets use the term 'ambiguity' to describe a virtue. They value the levels of meaning below the basic surface or the elemental response." He hopes, then, that the viewer of his photos will get the feel of what he's doing, will look again in a day or a week, or if the pictures are in a book, will be drawn to them once in a while, perhaps to see different dimensions.

The farm worker essay was shot on 35mm film. But Camhi tries to change the film or developer to match the needs of the subject. He tends not to think about technique as such. Having learned it, he believes, you no longer need to worry over it. You use it in the natural way you use nerve and muscle and bone when you walk.

He works mostly with the 35mm camera with a 90mm focal-length lens. "But I'll change when change makes sense," he says. "I'll also go to another camera, anywhere from 2¼ x 2¼ to 4x5 or 8x10. But again, it all comes down to what it is I wish to say—that determines which camera, which film, which developer, and how the print will look."

About the print he says, "I think a hell of a lot about it. I do all my own printing. I'll be very fussy about it, and won't leave it till it's exactly right. It's hard to surrender the craft of printing to someone else. In fact, I haven't really ended speaking through my photographs until that print is done."

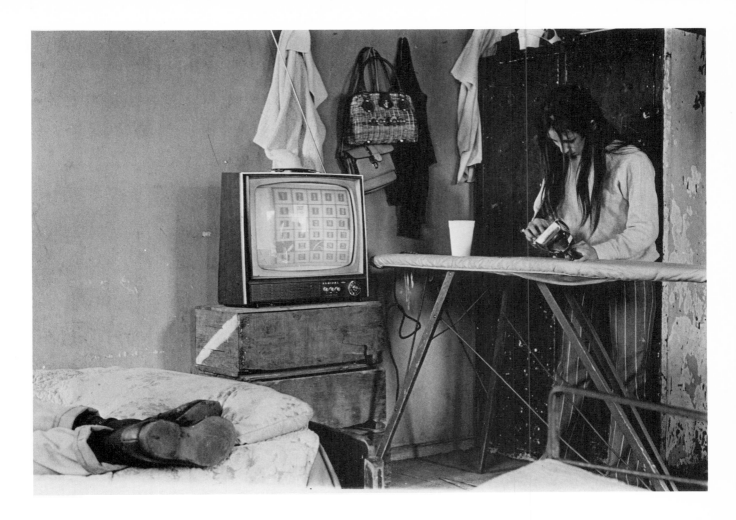

"Got it!"

MAKING YOUR OWN PHOTOGRAPHIC STATEMENT

Got it!'' Indeed he has. The camera has recorded the fact that he was there. When he returns home, he can display the collection of places where he and his wife took their holiday. He will derive much pleasure from these reminders, and perhaps so will his family and friends. This is one of the unique qualities of the camera—the ability to record the present moment and to act as an instrument for recalling the past. For the man looking at the cathedral it is all he wants from the camera. So it is for many people. As long as it gives them back a reasonable representation of where they have been and the sights they have seen, the camera has served its purpose.

There is nothing wrong with that. But for some people the camera must do more than help to induce nostalgia. What about the other possibilities lying quietly within that small lighttight box? There are so many hidden aspects of our lives and the world around us that can be revealed through the magic of the camera.

From the beginning of photography—more than one hundred and twenty-five years ago—it was obvious that the camera gave one a new way of seeing things. And the photographer soon began to realize that with this instrument he had the power not only to see but to comment on what he saw. He could go into places that one had only read or heard about and with the camera bring back records of what had moved him to awe, to tears, to anger. The camera became the means of making a personal statement.

If we want to use the camera to its full capacity, to have it convey what we feel about people, places, events, where do we start? What do we need in the way of equipment? What size camera, what kind of film?

Perhaps the best way to begin would be to study the photographs in this book and see what can be learned from them. What's clear as one goes from O'Sullivan to the modern photographers is the variety of cameras that were used. O'Sullivan's was a huge camera that required a sturdy tripod, his "film" a large plate of glass that he had to sensitize himself. Riis was not much better off. When going into some of the dingiest corners of the East Side, the dim cellars and dark backyards, he had to depend on magnesium powder to get the exposure he needed. Hine had the same problems for a long time, using glass plates and dragging them wherever his probing mind took him. Lange, though using the film base we are familiar with today, carried a 4x5 view camera for her work. The cameras used by the present-day photographers represented in this book are 35mms.

The important thing about the photographs in this book, then, is not so much what camera was used but the quality of the result. The value of these photographs would be considerably diminished if they were not sharp, if the tonal range were not so rich. The strength of the photographic statement varies with the photographer's command over the entire history of the photograph—from the initial mental click that saw the photograph and arranged it in the mind to its transfer to the camera and its passage through the laboratory to the final print. So techniques are important, but only in so far as they make effective what we have to say.

Note the directness with which all pictures in this book have been taken. No artifice, no tricks, are used; the prints are sharp, the statement unimpeded by clumsy technique.

If, as so many photographers feel, the small camera can best serve us, it is important to be aware of how careful we must be in using it. The very qualities that make it so attractive —small size, the number of exposures on one roll of film, interchangeability of lenses—pose a built-in danger. We must be exceptionally careful with the small camera to get the brilliant results visible in this book. Exposure, developing, printing—always demanding careful attention—must be especially meticulous processes if the best results are to be achieved.

Millions of people take photographs—but millions of people are not photographers. There is a wide gap between the man who "got it" and the person who wants to master what is needed to make effective photographs. If we are moved by the world around us and find the camera the tool to express our feelings, we must be prepared to learn the rules for achieving prints of the best quality, and then follow these rules no matter how tedious they seem or how tempting it is to try to bypass them. There are ways to get around some of the procedures— pushing the film speed and playing tricks with the developer —but these rarely result in the sort of beautifully detailed photographs contained in this book or in the published work of such masters as Paul Strand, Edward Weston, Eugene Smith, and Henri Cartier-Bresson. Learning the possibilities of the medium as well as its limitations, we can make the camera an eloquent voice for what we have to say.

One way to grow as a photographer is to look at the work of the best camera artists. Many books are available today that can give us not only hours of pleasure but also the opportunity to study what can be done with the camera when operated by a superb photographer. The quality of such work need not be discouraging; rather it should serve as inspiration and direction. Nobody who wants to write plays loses by reading Shakespeare.

The photographs in this book are a guide to what can be done with the camera. From the monumental themes of the Civil War and the Great Depression to the more limited but deeply moving subject of the rehabilitation of handicapped children, we can see how varied are the possibilities around us. Stop and think about the world you live in—your neighborhood, the people next door, what they do for a living, where they find their pleasures, how they meet their sorrows. One of the wonderful things about the camera is the way in which it discloses what was always present, but unobserved. Using the camera retrains the eye. Many things we once passed by, bored or blind, suddenly assume a special shape, a new character. Even our own backyard begins to look different as we see pictures in the way an old crate falls into an interesting shape against the wall or the way the afternoon sun slants over some chairs on the porch. With the camera we begin to sense our own personal response to that quality of light, that harmony of wood and stone. The camera connects us to the world around us. What could be more natural than to use it to discover the shape and mystery of that world?

And that world includes yourself—first of all, yourself. Few of us ever consider our own lives as an event. What we know of ourselves is too often what others tell us. No matter where we are or what we do, there is a life there to be explored. Our whole experience is available to us if we stop to think about it. The camera can be a means of discovery. There are no rules or restraints. Open yourself to new perceptions and you will find what you never before saw or realized. Your vision is not simply the surface of objects or people or events. It is what *you* feel about them, how *you* understand them. With your camera you are not just an observer; you are a participant. The world in all its forms becomes fresh and new, and you are its explorer.

Start exploring by making the camera your third arm. Carry it with you as much as possible—to school, to work, to the corner store. The man who "got it," like millions of others, uses the camera only a few times a year to record holidays and festive occasions. That's all he wants it to do, and he is satisfied. But you want more from it. The camera must be at work wherever you go because only in that way can you train your eyes to see and the camera to respond to what you perceive. Complete ease with the instrument can come only by using it constantly. Then the camera does what you want; there will be no barrier to saying what you have to say.

If, like the photographers in this book, you want to make your own statement about a social issue, a human problem, you need to establish a bond of understanding with the people you want to photograph. Start simply by examining your own feelings about what you intend to do, how you think about the situation you're concerned with, and the people at the heart of it. To be a concerned photographer means more than to be a camera-clicker, a walking encyclopedia of lenses and developers and filters. Knowing the camera is only part of the game, perhaps the lesser part; more important is understanding and feeling compassion for people.

There is no formula for success. Listening to lectures by experts may help; books may help (we hope this one does); studying the work of the great photographers will surely be useful. But ultimately, what you achieve is up to you, because you are unique; no one else can take your pictures or say what you want to say. Only you can do it.

FOR FURTHER READING

Titles marked with an asterisk (*) are available in paperback.

*Abbott, Berenice. *Berenice Abbott: Photographs.* New York: Horizon, 1970.
———. *The World of Atget.* New York: Weyhe, 1930.
Abramson, Michael. *Palante: Young Lords Party.* New York: McGraw-Hill, 1971.
*Brassai. *Brassai.* New York: Museum of Modern Art, 1968.
*Capa, Cornell, ed. *The Concerned Photographer I.* New York: Grossman, 1968.
*———. *The Concerned Photographer II.* New York: Grossman, 1972.
*Capa, Robert. *Photographs of Robert Capa.* New York: Grossman, 1969.
*Cartier-Bresson, Henri. *The World of Henri Cartier-Bresson.* New York: Viking, 1968.
Elliott, George. *Dorothea Lange.* New York: Museum of Modern Art, 1966.
Evans, Walker. *Walker Evans: Photographer for the Farm Security Administration, 1935–1938.* New York: Da Capo-Plenum, 1969.
Gardner, Alexander. *Gardner's Photographic Sketch Book of the Civil War.* New York: Dover, 1959.
Garven, Thomas H., ed. *Twelve Photographers of the American Social Landscape.* New York: October House, 1968.
*Gernsheim, Helmut and Alison. *Concise History of Photography.* New York: Grosset & Dunlap, 1965.
Goldsmith, Arthur, and Eisenstaedt, Alfred. *Eye of Eisenstaedt.* New York: Viking, 1969.
Gutman, Judith Mara. *Lewis W. Hine and the American Social Conscience.* New York: Walker, 1967.
Hine, Lewis W. *Men at Work.* New York: Macmillan, 1932.
Horan, James D. *Timothy O'Sullivan: America's Forgotten Photographer.* New York: Doubleday, 1966.

Hurley, F. Jack. *Portrait of a Decade: Roy Stryker and the Development of Documentary Photography in the Thirties.* Baton Rouge: Louisiana State University, 1972.

Lange, Dorothea, and Taylor, Paul Schuster. *An American Exodus: A Record of Human Erosion.* New York: Reynal & Hitchcock, 1939.

*Leavitt, Helen. *A Way of Seeing.* New York: Viking, 1965.

Life Editors, ed. *Documentary Photography.* New York: Time-Life, 1972.

————. *Photojournalism.* New York: Time-Life, 1971.

Lyons, Nathan. *Contemporary Photographers Toward a Social Landscape.* New York: Horizon, 1966.

Newhall, Beaumont. *History of Photography: From 1930 to the Present Day.* New York: Museum of Modern Art, 1964.

Newhall, Beaumont and Nancy. *Masters of Photography.* New York: Braziller, 1958.

Riis, Jacob A. *How the Other Half Lives* (with 100 photographs from the Riis Collection, Museum of the City of New York). New York: Dover, 1971.

Rothstein, Arthur. *Photojournalism.* 2nd ed. Philadelphia: Chilton, 1965.

Rothstein, Arthur; Vachon, John; and Stryker, Roy. *Just Before the War: Urban America from 1935 to 1941 As Seen by Photographers of the Farm Security Administration.* New York: October House, 1968.

Shahn, Ben. *Ben Shahn: Photographer.* New York: Da Capo-Plenum, 1969.

Smith, W. Eugene. *W. Eugene Smith: His Photographs and Notes.* New York: Aperture, 1969.

*Steichen, Edward. *The Bitter Years, 1935–1941: Rural America As Seen by Photographers of the Farm Security Administration.* New York: Museum of Modern Art, 1962.

*————, ed. *The Family of Man.* New York: Museum of Modern Art, 1955.

Strand, Paul. *Paul Strand: A Retrospective Monograph.* New York: Aperture, 1972.

————. *Mexican Portfolio.* 2nd ed. New York: Da Capo-Plenum, 1967.

Strand, Paul, and Newhall, Nancy. *Time in New England.* London: Oxford University Press, 1950.

*Szarkowski, John. *The Photographer's Eye.* New York: Museum of Modern Art, 1966.

*Taft, Robert. *Photography and the American Scene: A Social History, 1839–1899.* New York: Macmillan, 1938.

INDEX

ABOUT THE AUTHORS

Milton Meltzer, a specialist in graphic history and biography, has gained a wide reputation for his more than twenty-five distinguished books that reflect his deep interest in social reform. His *Pictorial History of Blackamericans,* written with Langston Hughes and C. Eric Lincoln is one of the most popular in its field, as are his pictorial biographies *Mark Twain Himself* and *A Thoreau Profile.*

Mr. Meltzer's work has earned many honors and awards. His biography of Langston Hughes was nominated for the National Book Award in 1969, and his book about the depression of the 1930s, *Brother, Can You Spare a Dime?,* won the Christopher Award. His three-volume documentary history of black Americans, *In Their Own Words,* won the Thomas A. Edison Award. Other notable works by Mr. Meltzer include his two-volume illustrated world history *Slavery* and a book on the Reconstruction period *Freedom Comes to Mississippi.*

Born in Worcester, Massachusetts, Mr. Meltzer was educated at Columbia University. He and his wife make their home in New York City. They have two daughters.

Bernard Cole has taught photography for many years, both in private and academic courses, and is now assistant professor in the art department of Brooklyn College.

As a working photographer, he has traveled widely throughout the United States, Mexico, and South America, covering stories in the sociomedical field for a variety of medical magazines and such organizations as UNICEF and International Planned Parenthood. Besides magazine publication, his photographs have appeared in several books, including the social documentary *The Bowery Man,* by Elmer Bendiner, and the *Pictorial History of Blackamericans,* by Langston Hughes, Milton Meltzer, and C. Eric Lincoln.

Photographs by Mr. Cole have twice appeared in "Photography in the Fine Arts" exhibits, which have toured museums in the United States and Canada, starting with a two-month stay at the Metropolitan Museum of Art in New York. He also recently had a one-man show at Shelter Island, New York.

Mr. Cole studied photography under Sid Grossman at the Photo League in New York City. He now lives in New York with his wife, Gwen; they have three children.